In Search of the Way

In Search
of the Way

Flora E. Wood

Radha Soami Satsang Beas

Published by:
Jagdish Chander Sethi, Secretary
Radha Soami Satsang Beas
Dera Baba Jaimal Singh
Punjab 143 204, India

Eighth edition 2003

10 09 08 07 06   8 7 6 5 4 3 2

ISBN 81-8256-136-1

Printed in India by: Lakshmi Offset Printers, Delhi-110092

Contents

Preface to the Seventh Edition

Mrs Flora E. Wood, the Master's representative in Britain, was born and lived in India for many years and learned of the teachings of the saints as a young woman in the early 1940s.

She was initiated by Maharaj Sawan Singh Ji and had the unusual opportunity to experience a close, personal association with both her own Master and, in the 1960s, Maharaj Charan Singh Ji. Back in those days—the 1940s and the early '60s—there were relatively few satsangis in the West, compared with the thousands who have been initiated since then. And of that small number, only a handful were able to spend time at the Dera. This book gives a first-hand account of those times when Mrs Wood and a small group of companions spent considerable time with the Master in informal discussions of Sant Mat and shared with him many intimate moments. In conveying her experiences, Mrs Wood communicates not only the teachings of the saints but also a little of how the Masters teach their disciples through the example of their own purity and love for God.

Mrs Wood has slightly revised this edition and has added an epilogue placing her account in a spiritual context from the vantage point of some thirty-two years later. With the growth of the sangat all over the world, the intimacy of those earlier days is no longer possible. But we also know that the true intimacy occurs spiritually, when we meet our Master's Radiant Form inside. His physical form is a means to that end.

In this account of a disciple's personal association with her Master, we share her joy in his presence. It may remind us of the union we all seek with our own Master, and how to go about making that union a reality.

Sewa Singh
Secretary

Radha Soami Satsang Beas
January 2000

Introduction

The river Beas, with its four companions—the rivers Jhelum, Chenab, Ravi and Sutlej—gives the Punjab its name *(panch aab,* five rivers) as a province of northern India. The Beas has held a significant place in the annals of India, both spiritually and politically. Early in the sixteenth century Guru Nanak, one of the greatest saints that India has produced, preached his message of Sant Mat, the Teachings of the Saints. Born at Talwandi, now known as Nankana Sahib, he settled and preached at Kartarpur Bedian, which lies on the west bank of river Ravi at a distance of about fifty miles from the present Radha Soami Colony on the bank of the river Beas, which will figure so largely in the following pages.

Over two hundred years before the birth of Christ, Alexander the Great, at the head of his hitherto victorious hosts, came to the banks of this waterway. Heavy clouds were gathering, and, before he could ford the shrunken stream, the monsoon broke in a great storm of lightning and rain, beating on the parched countryside and on the Himalayan heights nearby. The water from a thousand hills and streams filled the river basin and overflowed into the surrounding plain. Alexander's tired foot soldiers could not move in the thick clay morass, and this, aggravated by their long-standing homesickness and discontent, led to mutiny. Alexander, that great conqueror, had been outgeneralled by a river—the Beas. He turned back and a year later died on his journey homeward.

On the banks of this same river in the last years of the nineteenth century, Baba Jaimal Singh, the disciple of a well-known and loved saint, Soami Ji of Agra, had chosen, after thirty-four years as a devoted follower of his Guru, to serve his novitiate of mastership. In those days the country-side was sparsely populated and farmed by widely spaced villages, whilst the area around the river itself was a wilderness of scrub broken up by clefts of eroded clay. Undisturbed, he sat meditating for long hours at a time, as do all true Masters before taking up their great responsibilities. In the tree above him, he had secreted a bundle of chapatis and at long intervals he would arise and, taking one of the sun-dried unleavened cakes, would soak it in water, eat it and return at once to his devotions. It is said that he foresaw this spot becoming the nucleus of a spiritual activity which would radiate across the world.

He built a rough shelter from the rain and it was not long before he had a growing band of disciples. A well was sunk and buildings commenced in a modest way. The colony we know had started its course.

Subsequent to this, his successor Baba Sawan Singh Ji, after his accession to mastership, improved the colony to house the ever-growing number of his devotees. At his death in 1948, Sardar Bahadur Jagat Singh Ji, who followed him, and later Maharaj Charan Singh Ji, continued to alter and enlarge the existing site to cater to the periodic influx of literally thousands of disciples who come for instruction in Sant Mat—the philosophy they teach.

During my last visit to the colony, the idea occurred to me that a record written at the time and whilst events were fresh in the mind, might be of interest to the other British and Indian members of our party from England. Other sat-sangis who had not visited Beas might also share with us, vicariously, the blissful days we spent in our benign Master's company.

Since that time it was suggested that I enlarge this account to include earlier reminiscences: of how I met the Great Master, Maharaj Sawan Singh Ji, who initiated me; of how I was attracted by his teaching; and of the Dera in the days when I first studied Sant Mat.

The observations in the following pages are naturally inadequate reactions, of a purely personal nature, to rare and precious moments in the company of our beloved Satgurus. Here I am reminded of a story about a little boy who, in the garden of his cottage home, was playing with an old copper jug. It was a brilliant spring morning, fragrant and dewy, full of vital colour and sound, the drone of insects and the wild sweetness of birdsong. He sat for a long moment with a singing heart gazing into the sun-filled golden depths of his jug and thought with the unformulated loving thoughts of childhood, of his mother lying ill in the cottage in a comparatively dark room, and his heart suddenly ached to be able to convey some of the peace and beauty of the garden to her, for her comfort. He lay in the grass and thought: "If I leave the jug with its lid open for a little while, it will be full to the brim with sunlight." After some time he closed the lid and carried it carefully indoors to his mother and said: "I've brought you in some sunshine." But when he opened the jug, all was dark and cold within it, and sadness filled his heart.

Please give me your indulgence if my jug seems empty and inadequate.

PART I

EARLY MEMORIES: 1940–1946

When I took but two steps in the path of love,
Shorn was I completely
Of the distinction between belief and disbelief.

Bu Ali Qalandar

Early Memories

You ask me, dear Satguru, to recall how I was led to Sant Mat and to my Master, Hazur Maharaj Baba Sawan Singh Ji. In the past, my lack of good health was the indirect cause of notable friendships and happiness in my life; on that occasion it brought me the greatest experience anyone can have—that of meeting a true saint. As a therapeutic measure and to try and overcome the effects of a long illness, I applied in June 1940 for a secretarial appointment on the civil wartime staff of Army Headquarters, India, in Shimla. I was assigned to Colonel Sanders, whose secretary, a friend of mine, was about to be promoted. She aroused my interest by telling me that the Colonel was studying a form of mystical yoga. She could tell me little about it; and the Colonel, not long initiated himself, was not very communicative at first. What she did say intrigued me, however, as I had felt a deep sympathy during my twenty-eight years of life for the mystical beliefs of the country in which it had been my good fortune to spend my life. I had studied Buddhism and Theosophy to some extent, and the vegetarian ideal was by no means un-pleasing to my mind; thus I was partially prepared and waiting for enlightenment. A casual remark about the destination of a holiday Colonel Sanders was intending to take gave me the chance I had been eagerly awaiting, and I think he must have sensed in my questioning no idle curiosity, but a deep spiritual need which the Christian liturgical religion had never succeeded in satisfying. As a Protestant educated in a Catholic convent, I was critical of both religions and yet had absorbed from each those qualities which seemed to be most sincere: the simplicity and directness of the one and the devout dedication of the other. The ritualistic aspect left me unmoved, but the central figure of the Master, Christ, held my imagination. Coming to the philosophy of Sant Mat, however, made me aware for the first time of the principles behind my thinking.

Christ, though loved and revered as a perfect Master, seemed wrapped in the obscure confusion of the intervening centuries and was in this age deemed to be the only Son of God, born miraculously of a virgin. Hitherto in the physical sense this had raised a doubt in my subconscious mind. If God were all powerful, why would he need to upset the laws of nature which he himself had set in motion to produce, by miraculous physical means, an 'only' Son? What, anyway, was the significance of his being the *only* Son, when an all-loving omnipotent God had decreed that nature should reproduce itself and die over and over again, and that inherent in this system was an inability to carry a really vital memory from one generation to the next? How were preceding or succeeding generations to get the full impact of Christ's message, however divine he was, however powerful his teaching, however eloquent his biographers, if it were not given first hand? If mankind did not get this full impact, then God—

an otherwise loving God—was guilty of discrimination against these helpless, lost generations. If, as reputed, he were all-knowing, he would not revoke the methods of his own creation but would produce a perfect Son by natural means for each generation in turn. In no other way could his teaching be available to humanity for all times. Miraculous intervention would mean so much power wasted, for, although its drama would astound the bystander, it would not work a lasting cure in his inborn malady of ignorance, prejudice and egotism. Why, indeed, should God take such pains to be the physical father of this Son? All that really concerned the Son's disciples was the authenticity of his spiritual message, and an all-wise God concerned with their spiritual salvation would lay emphasis on this and not on the physical manner of his birth. Were not all men in all respects the product of God's will and therefore the sons of God? Their earthly fathers were essentially God's tools, his vehicle on this plane for their reproduction. Immediate physical paternity was of little consequence when viewed from a spiritual angle, for the whole contained the parts so completely that there should be no need to reassert his paternal association on an earthly level—everything eventually being of, or from, God.

This being so, I thought, every soul intent on salvation had an overriding responsibility to itself to prove that the means it chose for its salvation was absolutely authentic beyond a shadow of doubt. This could only be ensured by direct contact with a living Master, in person. In no other way could complete conviction be attained, for it is not the written word that convinces, nor even the spoken. It is only by observing the eyes and the sincerity of the voice that ultimate surety arrives and trust and love are born. A living personification of God was therefore required, one who would continually demonstrate his love tangibly, in the face of my own short-comings—who would point out a road to heaven, fashioned according to my own individual needs.

Hardly had I formed that desire mentally in a groping, wordless sort of way, when his emissary, the Colonel, ap-peared in my life and all that remained was to make a suit-ably graceful pretext to invoke his help. You may be sure I was not slow to seize this opportunity, and in a café, over in-numerable cups of tea and sandwiches, I ventured into this enthralling world of the spirit.

At first he described the colony at Dera Baba Jaimal Singh, presided over by a wise and benign teacher who did not ask one to change one's religion or way of life, other than by refraining from taking animal life in order to eat. This Guru, he informed me, gave one a course of study which one applied to one's life, of which the most important part was daily meditation. Since I had been an invalid and much on my own for long periods of my life, this appealed to me, for my thoughts had become introspective, though comfortable companions. No, he said, that was not enough; some striving was necessary to control and collect these thoughts at one point, a centre behind and between the physical eyes, known to mystics as 'the third eye' or *tisra til*. This was an optic with no physical location, which, given the opportunity, 'saw' a good deal better than the two with which I had been blessed at birth. It beheld in a manner impossible for earthly eyes, since it perceived a whole new and entrancing world within the compass of my head.

Again, this struck a sympathetic chord, for my body had failed me too often in the past for me to put much faith in its capabilities. So here I was, committed to a journey having no dimensions of time or space, to be seen not by sight but by perception within the confines of my own head, and to do this I must withdraw myself daily from the physical world for a set period of two-and-a-half hours. I must first close the nine doors, the portals of my body into the world— the eyes, ears, nostrils, mouth and lower bodily apertures— and steadily, unhurriedly and confidently withdraw the consciousness of life from the body and bring it up to await the Guru's appearance in his Radiant Form at the mystical third eye. Very well, what then?

"This alone will be difficult and will probably take some while", said the Colonel. "Try it for a time, whilst practising strict vegetarianism—no fish, meat nor eggs, nor any alcohol."

I was, of course, already familiar with the basic idea of those two interdependent axioms of all true teachings: karma and reincarnation. Karma or the law of cause and effect, I learnt now was, for practical purposes, subdivided into three kinds. The first kind consisted of some of our past good and bad credits and debits which were assigned for repayment in this present life—which were, indeed, the very fabric of every breath we took. Having repaid them, we automatically ceased to exist on this plane. Nothing could turn aside the repayment of this debt, but its effect could, and often was, mitigated by receiving initiation from a Perfect Master. It was known as *pralabdh* or fate karma.

The second kind of karma was known as *sinchit*. This was reserve karma, a surplus left over from past lives and was taken over by one's Master at initiation. It was, metaphorically, burnt; that is, it was consumed or absorbed at the time when, by the Master's divine assistance, one achieved full control over the mind. At this instant one emerged like a butterfly from a chrysalis into the realm of spirit. This, the Colonel said, was a moment of triumph, and, full of joy at the revelation of the experience, the soul cried out in a great voice, "Behold! I am soul!" *(Maiŋ aatmaa hooŋ!)*, which I always imagine, colloquially, to signify: "So *this* is what it means to be a soul! I am that!"—born of the tremendous upsurge of spirit needed to break through that last ceiling of the mind.

The third kind of karma, *kriyaman*, was new karma being made now with no impetus of the past impelling one to act, the results of which would be felt in the future.

The whole of the philosophy, or any true teaching, I was told, rested on three facts: the necessity for a living Perfect Master; that his teachings should indicate as their guiding principle the Sound Current or Audible Life Stream which the Bible calls the Word, Greek philosophers call Logos, Muslims name Ism-i-Azam or Kalam-i-Ilahi, and Indian saints call Shabd; and the necessity for contacting the divine Master through meditation within one's own body.

The perfect Guru was necessary to the searching soul as the supreme example by which to test its own progress at every stage. The Guru must be living, for otherwise one would get one's instructions second-hand; in other words, the power of an individual relationship would not exist, and personal problems could be resolved only by the application of generalizations. Each one of us was as unique as our own thumb impression, and therefore our spiritual training also was different in each case. The greatest of all reasons for a living teacher, however, was that this was a philosophy of devotion, or *bhakti,* and no true devotion is complete without a personal relationship on this plane. We were so lacking in spiritual imagination that unless we felt God had taken the trouble, personally, to contact us and to go on contacting us throughout our lifetime, we could not be entirely convinced that he cared enough. For this reason there was always a true saint available in the world for those who wished genuinely to find him. If their longing were deeply sincere, like the magnet and the needle, nothing, absolutely nothing, could keep them apart. He was made manifest in a bodily form for our assistance in the early stages on this plane so as to give us, by word of mouth, an inducement to go within our own body in meditation, when, after concentrating our whole being mentally at one spot between the eyes, we would transcend this earth life, or 'die whilst living', and encounter him in his Radiant Form within. Once we had done so, this form would never leave us during our whole journey to the infinite spiritual goal.

The Colonel explained the Sound Current as being at once my own life force and, in its greater aspect, the attribute of the Master within. It was capable of being heard—at first dimly, a mere reflection of its real, beautiful self—not with physical ears but from within one's own head. Though some people could catch this reflection before initiation, real contact with it could only come by accompanying the Radiant Form within after initiation from a true saint. We had lost conscious contact with the Current through possibly millions of lives of separation from it on these material levels, and only at the time of initiation did he give one the capacity for hearing it permanently again.

Due to one's karmic load one might not be able to distinguish the Sound Current immediately, but with practice and the lessening of the karmic load, the ability was gradually acquired of selecting it from the material sounds to which the mind was accustomed. Even then, its full compelling beauty was not heard, since one was still too near the world, too confused with karmic attachments. However, with rigorous and dedicated practice one trained the muscles of the spirit and eventually gained inner perception of its full cadence. If it were realized that all worldly sounds were the result of some activity, then one could think of this not as an effect but as a cause, the Primal Cause.

He said that when the true Sound was contacted later in one's meditative practice, it was of such a compelling and entrancing quality that those who heard it found it difficult to return to the physical plane.

He also stressed the necessity for striving towards moral rectitude in all things, for one should "cleanse the vessel before filling it". In this respect one had five enemies which must be subdued, the five passions that assailed us through our senses: lust, anger, greed, undue attachment to worldly things and ego *(kam, krodh, lobh, moh, and ahankar)*. Until the regions of the mind were left behind, one would be constantly enticed or assailed by these remorseless enemies. Neither confidence nor weakness hindered their onslaught, for they were the weapons of the negative power (Kal) that ruled the material planes—a power whose duty it was to ensure that a soul remained within the wheel of reincarnation, the cycle of birth, death and birth, over and over again. Each one of these passions was a deadly enemy, but the worst of all, the one indeed that inspired and fed on all the others, the last to leave us, was ego.

Meeting My Master

When I first spoke of Sant Mat to my parents, they were dismayed, thinking I would lose strength with little or no animal protein in my diet. I was unwilling to antagonize them for I felt that if patience and restraint were exercised, they would be so persuaded of the sincerity of my convictions as to realize that no harm could come to me.

In the meantime, the Colonel had arranged for me to spend a part of the Christmas holidays at Beas with Mrs Johnson, an American disciple living at the Dera. Before this, however, I was destined to meet my dearest Master for the first time when he visited the Colonel's house in New Delhi, to which city our office and my family had moved for the cold weather season. No words of mine can describe my eager anticipation on that clear sunny October afternoon at the office. The Colonel had gone ahead to meet his guest and later he telephoned to say that the Master wished me to come to him. Riding to the house on my bicycle, I felt as though I were flying on air down the Secretariat slope. This, I thought, is how it feels, this rapturous ecstasy of return to meet the Master from whom your soul has been separated for perhaps as many as eight million, four hundred thousand different species of lives. At last I arrived and there he was, impeccably dressed, an upright stately figure with a long snow-white beard and high turban and a countenance of quiet dignity, smiling into my eyes and holding out his hand, with a deep "Hallo" of greeting. While he shook my hand and I murmured a conventional reply, my mind felt as though it was metaphorically bowing at his feet. It is strange how we contain ourselves at such a time when our inner selves leap and dance for all the world like an exultant puppy greeting a much loved master after a long separation.

The Master replied to my eager enquiry for initiation that this could only be given to one who was wholly vegetarian, but he told me to continue practising meditation assiduously in the meantime and to use temporarily as *simran* the words *Radha Soami.** Simran, he explained, literally means 'remembering'. During the course of our daily lives, he said, we use this method in a worldly sense to concentrate our minds on what we are doing by thinking constantly of it. In order to detach our minds from earthbound thinking and

---

* This advice pertains to the particular disciple to whom it was given and cannot be applied as a general rule.

direct them into spiritual channels, the Masters utilize this simple natural habit and encourage their disciples to use it, whenever they can, at all times when the mind is not actively engaged in worldly work. When the habit becomes automatic, one finds that simran will continue subconsciously even when the mind is concentrating physically. Then, when the disciple comes to practise his meditation, to some extent his mind will already be oriented towards spiritual planes. Simran is also used as the first stage of meditation to assist the disciple to withdraw his consciousness from the world, to close the bodily apertures, and to lift the attention to the *tisra til* between and behind the physical eyes. The need for simran ceases only when the inner Radiant Form of the Master is contacted, but can be used to test the validity of any inner experience. Simran can also be of assistance to steady the mind and as a means of spiritual protection at any moment of danger or stress, for it has all the power of the Master behind it. He assured me that the words Radha Soami would take a soul up to the top of the mental plane, but the simran words given at the time of initiation, when the Master linked the soul with the Sound Current, transcend the realm of the negative power and connect it with the highest realms of the spirit.

Maharaj Ji also recommended the careful study of existing books in English (which at that time consisted only of Dr Johnson's writings, *Mysticism—The Spiritual Path* by Professor L.R. Puri, and Soami Ji's *Sar Bachan)* and seeking satisfactory answers to all questions uppermost in my mind.

A few weeks later I left for Beas on holiday.

Elizabeth Bruce Johnson

The Dera in those days (except on the occasion of *bhan-daras* or monthly satsangs) was a quiet little collection of brick buildings centred around a main quadrangle. A rough cinder track led to it from the railway station-cum-village of Beas about three miles to the south on the main north-western railway that connected Delhi with Lahore and the North-West Frontier of India, as it then was before the partition of India and Pakistan. On three sides, fields of wheat, sugar cane and other cereal and vegetable crops stretched, for in this respect the free kitchens of the Dera were almost entirely self-supporting, even at the time of the largest meetings. On the fourth side, the river Beas ran much as it does today. To the north-west, the Himalayas seemed to float in a blue haze above the river and the plain. Living conditions were very simple for the two or three Westerners who were there at any one time, but they found it adequate and restful with an irre-sistible rustic charm all its own. They were usually housed in the old guest house facing the river or had a room in Dr Johnson's house.

At the time of my first visit, the doctor (a well-known American medical practitioner who had lived permanently with his wife at the Dera and had lent his skillful services as both physician and surgeon free for the purpose of seva) had passed away not long before. His widow continued to live there, practising her considerable skill as a herbalist. She had, however, unfortunately contracted severe dysentery and was very weak and ill while I was there. Normally she prepared her own meals but this had become increasingly difficult, and trained help was almost unobtainable in this isolated spot. For a time we considered the possibility of my being her companion-housekeeper and nurse, but this proved impracticable. The Master in his wisdom knew she only had a short while to live. I shall never forget the quality of those days spent in her company. She was a tall, spare woman with red-gold hair. One would not have called her good-looking but there was a slow refined grace about her and, for want of a better word, I can only describe as an aura around her, engendered by her intense and transparent adoration of the Master. She seemed to know instinctively when he was near and, shedding the lethargy of her illness, she would move quickly, walking with radiance shining from her face to greet him, or just stand while he passed on his way for a walk or to inspect some work proceeding nearby.

"Never turn away from a Master's approach", she would instruct me. "Every step towards him removes untold karma."

I was avid for knowledge and questioned her interminably, much to her delight. When we sat together late of an evening and came to the end of a line of thought, I would see her bright eyes looking quizzically across at me (the room being lit by the intimate soft glow of an oil lamp), as if urging me to still further efforts of enquiry. The lamp would not be lit at the first fading of the light, and I would sit and she would lie, her long slender form wrapped in a Kashmiri ring shawl of wool, soft as silk and creamy white in colour. As dusk fell and the enchanting scent of that little garden shrub, 'the Lady of the Night' (which in memory, for me, forever

sheds its sweet perfume on the Indian night) would drift in
through the open window, I would be aware only of her eyes,
large and shining with love and full of vitality in her poor,
wasted inert body, as she told me of the glory and beauty of
her Master or of those regions to which she was soon to slip
away. Though we had known each other for so short a time,
we both felt a warm companionship between us which must
have taken many lives to engender. How rightly Dr Johnson
called her 'The Unquenchable Flame'—the name so aptly
described her—for after a time the dim room seemed to fall
away and under the spell of her words we seemed to be in
another world of spiritual enlightenment so pervaded with
love that it glowed with a soft radiance, moving through a
universal heaven of stars and moonlight, out to where, in a
garden that beggared the Hesperides, we went walking hand
in hand to meet the Radiant Form of our beloved Master.

Satsang

In the morning of each day we would breakfast simply.
Then having covered our heads with a scarf or veil in defer-
ence to the Eastern custom, in common with the handful of
satsangis then living at the Dera, we would converge on the
main courtyard to await the Master's arrival for satsang. In a
few minutes, with their voices greeting him with hymns of
praise, he would walk slowly and majestically from the door-
way of his house (he was then, in the autumn of 1940, eighty-
two years of age), with his long shining white beard and

aquiline features, a stately upright figure, outstanding in the crowd that surrounded him. He would be clothed, if the weather were cold, in a beautiful cream coloured, or sometimes a beige Gilgiti *choga*—a loose-sleeved coat reaching to the ankles and richly braided around the collar and down the chest.

What magnificence was there in that face, and yet what a calm kindly dignity: the face, one might feel of God the Father, such dependability and trust it engendered in one; a fearless eye, sometimes piercing in quality but when alighting on some fortunate person—perhaps talking to his neighbour unaware of his gaze—full of gentle, caressing love. At such moments I used to think how much and how often we take his loving care for granted.

The Master's satsangs were delivered with quiet effortless assurance in a voice whose timbre it is difficult to describe, but whose tones float across the years to me as bells might carry clearly across a valley—bell-like is perhaps the best description one could give them. There was absolutely nothing of self-awareness in his bearing and yet it flooded that courtyard as that of no earthly dignitary. The memory of those satsangs seems so full of gaiety and laughter. The Master often interspersed the discourses with parables, frequently of a humorous nature, and he would chuckle and laugh till the tears came into his eyes. In the words of the Persian poet-Master Jami, I used to feel:

> ...Sitting in the shadow of the Perfect,
> His soul found quiet; sweet it seem'd

Sweeping the chaff and litter from his own,
To be the very dust of Wisdom's Door.

In the spring and autumn of every subsequent year and during the Christmas holidays I would go to the Dera for the few days of leave the war allowed us, to refresh my jaded spirit. Sometimes Colonel Sanders and Sir Colin Garbett, a South African initiate, were there, and in later years their colleague and a subsequent initiate, Colonel Martin, joined us as well. I also came to know the royal family of Sangli and the Rajwade ladies.

An occasion I clearly remember was in the company of Rani Lakshmibai Rajwade (who was present later at my initiation). She and I gathered red roses and jasmine on our way to visit Maharaj Ji with some of her household, in the little rooftop courtyard in his house. She bowed at his feet and presented him with the flowers. He took them and laughingly scattered them over us as we sat around him. Of course everyone scrambled joyously to possess some of the now-precious flowers; the scene was one of merry colour and bright faces. I have my rose and jasmine petals, treasured to this day, even now full of rare scent.

On another occasion, soon after I had been commissioned into the Army, I arrived at the Dera after the small evening satsang had begun, in my new uniform—very proud of its neat cut and newly twinkling badges of rank. The Master looked towards me, interrupted what he was saying and with a playful smile he chaffed me, "Oho! She has become an officer!" to the good-humoured and affectionate

The Great Master and his son, Sardar Harbans Singh, with Sir C. Garbett and Col. C. W. Sanders.

Maharaj Charan Singh holding satsang at Beas.

laughter of the small gathering. I can still remember the glow of pleasure and love as of a welcoming father and family, given me that far-off day by my beloved Master and his sangat.

The Inner Journey

During the course of a satsang, the Master once described the journey one would travel within. He began by explaining that, when we try to express ourselves on this plane, we use words and writing, facial expressions and the like, to convey our meaning to each other. When, however, we begin to go within, we find ourselves perceiving directly. The result of this is an increase in our powers of discernment on this plane, and earthly methods of communicating become increasingly inadequate. This means that any description of our inner exaltation must be inadequate. The further we proceed, the more difficult it becomes to convey the sheer spiritual transport we experience. Just as the written word is not as expressive as the spoken word, with all the nuances of facial expression and gesture to give it its true emphasis, inner experiences are far more rich in spiritual significance than those of this earthly body. It is for this reason, I suppose, that earthly descriptions of internal transport sound inadequate, whereas a pointer is really being used, which will act as a simple indication to the traveller on this path that he is on the right way and that will, at the same time, have as universal a validity as possible for all who read or hear it, (much as a map, though not fully resembling the countryside, nor conveying its true atmosphere, can act as a working guide to it).

At all events, in the early stages of the spiritual journey, each one approaches their goal bringing a different mentality to bear on their surroundings as they go, so that an average has to be struck which all will recognize clearly. The parlance of each successive plane seems incomprehensible to those below. This barrier is necessary, for every soul on the path must work individually and deserve his entry into, and understanding of, each region. Moreover, those in higher planes recognize the parlance of lower planes and appreciate the necessities which fashion them, but this is not so in reverse. To those on lower planes, the language and usages of higher planes is incomprehensible until they rise into them.

The Master drew a simple simile to illustrate this: A young child beginning his school life would not understand how to solve a problem in higher mathematics, but to an advanced student, addition and subtraction would offer no problem. When making spiritual progress, however, a paradox occurs, for those minds not over-encumbered with intellect find their way more quickly than agile minds, for love of the Master makes them interested, not in the means but in the end. To them nothing is impossible or absurd if he has declared it to be possible.

We were told that whilst repeating the words (simran) given to us at initiation, having concentrated our attention at the third eye and broken through the dark veil that obscures the path in the first stages, we step out as through a window.

We appear to go through the brightness of the sun and the moon, where at a point known as the Eight-Petalled Lotus (Asht Dal Kanwal) we are very lovingly welcomed by the refulgent form of the Radiant Master (his *nuri sarup).* This is a moment of the deepest significance to the disciple for he begins to understand and accept the workings of his fate karma *(pralabdh)* and to be content with the manner of its repayment. Also the Sound Current (Shabd) becomes stronger and its power of attraction exerts a magnetism on the attention of the satsangi to such an extent that he now finds it as difficult to stay out in the world of phenomena as before he found it difficult to go in. Most important of all: from this point the Master's Radiant Form never leaves his disciple until the highest plane is reached. Simran is held in abeyance whilst the Radiant Master is visible to the disciple, and they proceed through this sub-astral plane piercing the brightness of the stars and reaching the astral zone known as Sahansdal Kanwal or the Thousand-Petalled Lotus. This is a mental transforming station where the power which supplies all lower planes is both stored and generated. It appears to radiate an unearthly light like that of a thousand candles, or a flame with a thousand tongues, so penetrating and refulgent that it warrants its descriptive name; time and space seem of less significance here. The soul meets the Lord of this region and satsangis see him bow down before their Master in homage— this is true of each successive ruler.

Again they journey on and reach another and vaster power centre of universal or causal mind called Trikuti.

This also has its ruler or nucleus. These two regions (Sahansdal Kanwal and Trikuti) with their millions of worlds and universes constitute the heaven of most established religions.

Now even the idea of time and space ceases to exist, for on leaving this plane the satsangi sheds his mind, as lower down he shed his body—it is no longer needed in the plane he is now to experience. It is here that the naked soul, freed of all karmic trappings, suddenly realizes its own power and glory and recognizes its complete identity with all creation and the uncreated element it is entering. It has, to some degree, through its intense devotion, begun the actual merging process with the Almighty, and this proceeds apace as it penetrates the successively bright conditions it now experiences. Time and space, dark and light, good and bad, all the pairs of opposites which are the hallmarks of the mind are recognized as the illusions they really are, and are left behind, for there is no longer duality of being, no longer 'me' and 'thee'. As it progresses, less and less effort is required, for not only is there less material resistance on successive planes, but individuality is being disseminated and union with all other souls is imparting confidence and surety. Paradoxically, that is why the human being is spoken of as 'the top of all creation' for it is in human form that the greatest efforts have to be made. Far more energy is used comparatively in the first few inches a locomotive moves in hauling a train than at any other time in its journey.

This region is known as Daswan Dwar (the Tenth Door) and its light is indescribably bright and increases in intensity and beauty as one proceeds. Having gained this spiritual plane, still somewhat admixed with matter, the soul begins to traverse a dark and fathomless abyss where souls who have lost their way are apparently hampered from onward progress. They are blissfully satisfied with their condition, however; but only those accompanied by a saint of the first magnitude ever find their way across this immense void. It is of such utter darkness that although the soul here has its own light equal to the light of twelve of our suns, it cannot cross this darkness without the light of the Satguru.

Higher still on the threshold of the final stage is the region known as Bhanwar Gupha. From here the soul gets its first glimpse of the final stage and this instant it automatically realizes its complete identity with that glorious Being and with all else, and cries out, "I am God!" *(Maiŋ aatmaa hooŋ)*.

Finally, still in the company of the Guru, we enter the ultimate heaven, Sach Khand, where the Master's duty is complete for we are now one with the Lord of that region, a great ocean of light into which the drop of our being becomes merged. This plane is without end but appears to recede into brighter and brighter regions each purer than the last. Names for them are given to us for our guidance such as the Invisible Realm, the Inaccessible Realm and the Nameless Realm—Alakh Lok, Agam Lok and Anami Lok—to distinguish them on this plane, but the Master explained that they beggar description.

The final and all-pervading stage is known as Radha Soami Dham—the Abode of the Lord of the Soul—this, the Master said, was all love, nothing but unalloyed bliss and an indescribable purity of love, for the soul has, for all eternity, united with the Lord.

Dera Friends

The Master spoke little English but we often conversed with such notable satsangis as Sardar Bhagat Singh, Professor Jagmohan Lal, Bibi Rakhi—a wise old lady, who attended upon the Master's personal needs—and Rai Sahib Harnarayan, who was at that time his secretary, and very fortunate we were, for all except Bibi Rakhi spoke fluent English. We also had long interviews with Sardar Bahadur Jagat Singh Ji, later to be chosen as my Master's successor. Before retirement he had been a professor of chemistry and later vice-principal at Lyallpur Agricultural College.

He told us that all the Masters of the first magnitude have been noted for the fact that they never under any circumstances accept money for their personal use. All money accepted by them is only used for the benefit of the community as a whole, but they themselves live only on money they have earned during their working life, or have private incomes of their own. He said that by the same token, a true Master always encourages his disciples to earn their living and not to live on the charity of others, as is so often the case in India when a person is seeking religious enlightenment.

Comparatively few people are permitted to stay at the Dera indefinitely. The majority of permanent residents are retired people with sufficient incomes to maintain themselves independently, who are there for a practical reason—to render service in various ways, without worldly recompense. This service is done for the benefit of the vast community that assembles at the time of the four bhandaras held annually to commemorate the birth or death of one of the recent Masters, during the monthly satsangs, or to help with the overseas and inland correspondence whereby those away from the Dera keep in direct communication with the Master, and in many other forms as the need arises.

Initiation

Before I left Beas, Mrs Johnson arranged an interview with Maharaj Ji during which she made a strong representation that except for the diet problem, I was in every other way quite ready for initiation! In high good humour she rallied the Master, begging that I be given at least one of the five names granted at initiation. He was greatly amused at her ingenuous demand. With affection for her shining in his eyes (he had bestowed on her the epithet Gur Piari—Beloved of the Master), he laughingly said, "If I give her one, I may as well give her all five!" to which she quickly responded,

"Then give her all five!"

"But she is still eating meat", he replied.

"Never mind, that is not her fault! She doesn't want to

eat it", she pleaded whilst I stood by, begging with my eyes for all I was worth.

"Very well, when I pass through Delhi later on we shall see", he said, seeming to relent. And so it came to pass, but Beloved of the Master had by then been gathered by the Master for his heavenly garden. She passed away in February in the hospital at Lahore and in March the Master, once more visiting Colonel Sanders' bungalow in Delhi, bade me attend him there and I had the five names given to me.

During the following summer, having contracted a form of fibrositis, I consulted a doctor who, I knew, would prescribe a meatless diet as a part of the cure. My parents met the new approach with a twinkle in their eyes. My mother remarked, "You are very much in earnest about this philosophy, aren't you?" and indicated they would no longer obstruct my wishes if the treatment did not affect my health adversely. Of course the experiment was successful as I was prescribed a carefully balanced and wholesome diet—an introduction to vegetarianism few people experience.

Whilst on leave in October, I journeyed to Beas with the Colonel for the second part of my initiation to which there was now no obstacle. This was the more significant half of the instruction—the true initiation when the Master actually links the soul with the Sound Current.

I well remember an agonizing repayment of karma made twenty-four hours beforehand, perhaps one of the most disabling migraine headaches I had ever suffered. The Colonel and dear Rani Rajwade had practically to carry me into the

Master's presence that day of days—but with what exaltation of spirit, I will not here enlarge upon!

I often marvel at the ease with which he absorbed me into his fold—the first British woman, young and reserved, to seek initiation at his hands. He fitted me most naturally into his scheme of things, sponsored (for my parent's comfort) by an officer of the same service to which my father belonged, entertained by a kindly American woman who treated me with the greatest affection from the moment we first met, and godmothered by a charming and cultured Indian lady who gave me support during my final initiation. What love you bestowed on me, my beloved Master, in even the smallest detail of my advent to your feet!

During the course of the same year Rai Sahib Harnarayan, Maharaj Ji's secretary, had passed to a better life. In accordance with custom, when a year had elapsed, a memorial service was held in the main hall of the colony, the satsang ghar, presided over by the Master. Colonel Martin had joined Colonel Sanders and myself at the Dera and we all three attended the service. It was a bright afternoon and the sun streamed in through the open doors. Not many people were present, only the basic staff usually resident at the Dera and a few Indian visitors. Later we compared our reactions, and all to whom we spoke felt the same sense of elation and transport. The scene, already colourful and bright, seemed to take on added intensity as though a rainbow had been thrown over it all. Each one's face appeared as though it glowed with health and happiness and the Master was suffused with a kind of nimbus of bright sunshine and colour—not unnaturally so, but as though all accustomed processes of life had been increased well beyond the usual mortal bounds. A radiant feeling of happiness remained after we left the hall and continues to this day in my memory.

At the end of this holiday I had to return to duty earlier than my companions. In those days, as you may remember, dear Master, the train seldom stopped at Beas on its journey from Lahore to Delhi, and to ensure my berth it was necessary to go by slow train to Lahore and to board the Frontier Mail from there. This entailed leaving Beas in the early evening before satsang had finished. I had Maharaj Ji's previous permission to slip away quietly when the time came and accordingly at the appointed moment rose to do so. Hazur paused in what he was saying and, smiling at me, said, "Why do you want to hurry away?" Seeing my troubled look—nonplussed as I was at this unexpected invitation—he said gently, "Very well, you had better go." I left, but what was my chagrin when, with myself aboard, the fast train to Delhi drew to an unscheduled halt on arriving at Beas station from the direction of Lahore and stopped quite long enough to have allowed me to have boarded it in comfort. Indeed I could sorrowfully visualize myself coming in at the compartment door as I would have done had I shown instant faith by taking the Master at his word! I hope I have learned from this to be completely and immediately flexible in his hands, at any given moment, when he indicates a line of action or thought, however improbable it may seem.

A New Life

In 1943 Colonel Sanders left for the United Kingdom on retirement. I continued to visit the Dera as frequently as my responsibilities would permit but, as these were increasing due to the intensified war effort in South-East Asia, the length and number of visits were necessarily reduced. In 1945 after the war ended, my health deteriorated once more and I was strongly advised by the doctors that it would be detrimental to my health to continue living in the East. Accordingly I was to be discharged on medical grounds from army service in the United Kingdom.

In January 1946 I visited the Dera for the last time for many years. The Master received me there with great love and affection. He seemed most solicitous as to my future and enquired as to the chances of accommodation in England, which due to the war and its aftermath were a very real problem at that time. He also expressed the hope that the satsangis in England would welcome me with love and kindness when I reached there, just as a loving father would, who felt anxious as to the welfare of his daughter.

I saw him once more, in Delhi, before I sailed in April 1946, to take leave of him. Kneeling before him I asked for his blessing and he gave me such a perceptive look that made me realize how fully he understood the turmoil in my heart. I felt I was leaving home and country for an uncertain future with inadequate health, but most of all, never again might I see his physical form and hear his loving voice advising and instructing me. He placed his hand gently for an instant on my shoulder. Dear Beloved! All the bells in heaven rang for me at that moment!

Problems

During early investigations into Sant Mat, certain aspects of it puzzled me. Their importance loomed unduly large at the time. The answers given were reasonable, but did not fill me with conviction. Since then I have found that other people have experienced the same difficulties on first approaching the philosophy. Through attending satsangs, reading books or as a result of meditation, I have since found solutions that have completely satisfied me. One of my problems might act as a prototype, as its answer illustrates the whole situation well.

It was: Whether or not we can really exercise free will. The whole concept of modern life in the West is based upon competition. It dominates one's education, home life and work; it pursues one through life and sets all one's standards. To succeed in our highly integrated society, one is taught to be superlative at one's pursuits, to be an individualist—different from all the other millions of one's kind whilst still conforming; success in life depends upon it. This difference can only be achieved by an effort of will—the greater the success, the stronger the effort. On coming to Sant Mat however I found the situation reversed. One had to train oneself to give up attachment to worldly success and submit one's will to the Guru. Before I fully understood this, I thought any

new goal could be wrested from the infinite by sheer determination and will power, and having gained the final splendid
goal, what a waste it would be for that highly trained individuality to be swamped in an ocean and become undifferen-
tiated! I wanted to be a person, to experience all this as 'me'.
As a British woman I was proud of my birthright of indepen-
dence and reserve. When I looked at some of my contempo-
raries I felt: One could carry this business of merging too far!

Of course the latter thought soon disappeared when I
considered that karma entirely influences personal relation-
ships up to the point where the mind is finally relinquished,
and once one is above its influence, both attractions and re-
pulsions vanish and all become as radiant and perfect as the
good Lord with whom we are seeking to merge ourselves.

But what of free will? This, I thought is a more funda-
mental quality and a desirable one. My mind was appeased
however, by the injunction that obedience to a perfect Master
was the most desirable attribute of a good satsangi. This is
the best solution when we are perplexed in the early stages,
for answers come very often unsought, later—full conviction
always dawning in the wake of love. It was not however till
much later that I had the answer, very ably explained in
Professor L.R. Puri's book *Mysticism—The Spiritual Path*,
Volume I. This two-volume book is a good commentary on
the Indian approach to spirituality and helps the Westerner
to understand much that the Indian takes for granted from
birth. He states:

If man has 'free will', then it means that he can choose
between various alternatives, and as long as the choice is thus

open, it is undecided and unsettled, it is uncreated…. It is known to none, not even to God; for if God knows it, it means that it is already fixed and the man has no choice. Thus if man has 'free will' none can have foreknowledge. These two things, God's foreknowledge and man's free will seem to be incompatible…. Thus to all appearances it seems that either God has foreknowledge, or man has free will. Both things cannot 'be' at the same time. If they are, then it is a great and important problem for us to know how such obvious contradictions can be reconciled. What sort of God do we have, who knows what we are doing and what we shall do, and still leaves it to our free choice to do whatever we like, and what sort of creatures must we be?

Later he answers his question thus:

We can say that reality has grades…at the last stage it is in its absolute truth…. The phenomena of each plane are true for that plane; it is the same order of truth as the existence of that plane, but in the truer and more penetrating light of the next higher plane, this truth loses its validity and force….

Now on this plane, does this world exist or not? Well… with the transcendent insight of mystic transport we find that …this world ceases to exist as a physical world nor do we have any existence as men…but this final truth cannot come into the mind of man so long as he is on the human level; because in absolute reality neither he exists nor his mind as such…. How then can true knowledge come into a delusive unreal mind…. For the mystic of the absolute stage reality is the transcendent One; for us it is this world of manyness. He embraces absolute reality; we grope in relative reality or appearance.

This also settles the question of the free will of man and the foreknowledge of God. Both can appear to be true at the same time for they are truths of different grades of reality.... Thus in absolute truth, man has no existence as man and consequently his free will is also non-existent, or rather the question of his free will does not arise...our existence as men and our free will are realities of the same order. They are real, relative to each other, but unreal in absolute truth.... The absolute reality is truly one but it is not for men to say so; for they can never know it so long as they are human. It is only the superhuman insight of mystic transport that reveals reality as the transcendent absolute One.

As for the determination to succeed, it is the effect of devotion to a cause. Sometimes in meditation it is misplaced, for one can try too hard with nerve and muscle—with one's physical body, to enter mental and spiritual planes, resulting in pain to the physical body and a singular lack of spiritual progress. Meditation should be embarked upon in a relaxed attitude of both body and mind. One is, of course, learning to relax completely and not interpose one's own will but to give up action and hand oneself over entirely to the Master's will. Herein lies the unique boldness and strength of this philosophy, for otherwise it would be impossible to relax one's ego so completely as to hand oneself over entirely to anyone but God incarnate. Nevertheless, it is only by so doing that self can be entirely subdued by perfect devotion. And only God incarnate could give one everything, but *everything,* in return; to the extent of merging one completely with the Supreme Power.

PART II

THE RETURN: 1961–1962

Slaves we are, and unencumbered,
Best may do the Master's mind;
And, whatever He may order,
Do it with a will resigned.

Jami, *Salaman and Absal*

The Return

As the sangat in England increased its membership, both by the initiation of British people interested in its teachings and by immigrant Indian satsangis in large numbers, the idea of a party visiting the Dera by air grew in our imagination. A few individual members had been able to put this into practice but it was not until August 1961 that Gurchetan Singh, the sponsor of the Indian group, presented the idea of an expedition to the Dera by air during the following winter season. Having received the blessings of our present Satguru, Maharaj Charan Singh Ji,[*] on the scheme, Gurchetan, with help from other members of the Indian group, was able to organize the visit so that we all left together on Christmas Day but returned, each one at their own convenience.

Our party consisted of seven British members and thirty Indians, not all of whom were initiates. The British satsangis were Mrs Margaret Benson-Cooke, Mrs Eleanora Jepp, Mrs May Holt, Mr Alex McCaskill, Mr Claud Lovelace, my husband Ronald and myself. Three Indian members who also

---

[*] Maharaj Charan Singh passed from his physical form on June 1, 1990, after appointing the present Master, Baba Gurinder Singh, as his successor.

went were Gurchetan himself, Mr R. Kareer and Mr Har-
mandir (Mohindar) Ahuja.

25th December

Today at 9:30 a.m. our party assembled at Great Cum-
berland Place, the sangat's London centre and from there we
travelled by chartered coach to London Airport. Although
the morning was icy, Colonel Sanders came out to wish us
"Godspeed!" and many Indians accompanied us as far as the
airport to see us away. When we arrived there, a slight mist
began to form, but it soon dispersed; we took off on time
and all was well, our aircraft being a Comet 4c. Jet.

26th December

We had an uneventful journey touching down at Rome
just before sunset, and after dark at Cairo and Doha, arriving
at Karachi by 10:35 a.m. Some hours later, having changed
airlines, we proceeded to Delhi, hoping to arrive at 5 p.m.

Later, after considerable delay with the customs authori-
ties, which lost us our train to Beas, we went to a supper provided by a satsangi railway official at the main Delhi station.
He arranged sleeping accommodation for us.

27th December

This morning we continued our travels by train. We
reached Beas soon after dark, where we were joyfully reunited
with friends who came to meet us at the station, including
Maharaj Ji's wife, Harjit, and Mrs Bea Jauncey, one of our
number who had preceded us to India earlier in the season.

There was plenty of transport for all: a bus to carry the Indian satsangis, a lorry for all our baggage, and we brought up
the rear in Maharaj Ji's car.

When we arrived at the Dera, Mohindar (who was a
friend of the Master's since childhood) organized a procession at the front entrance. We all went through the lamplit
dusk, the Indians singing the *benti* hymn,[*] through the main
courtyard (where, feeling slightly light-headed from the joy
of my return combined with fatigue, the surroundings seemed
like a vaguely remembered experience in another region), out
through the further gates and under the archway into the
Master's beautiful garden. There it lay, his house, glowing
with light at the end of the drive, down which we went, singing more softly as we stood on its steps. We were welcomed
inside and waited a short time in the lounge until he came
and sat with us. Mohindar introduced us one by one and
Maharaj Ji just sat there, quietly smiling and nodding, with
an expression of ineffable love on his face and we felt all the
fatigue of the journey fall from us.

28*th* December

People are beginning to arrive for the bhandara and so
satsang (delivered in Punjabi) was held in the spacious courtyard of the satsang ghar. One of the points Maharaj Ji made
was that when we are initiated we are given two legs with
which to walk to Sach Khand. The first leg is that of simran
(repetition), and when we have learnt to put that firmly for-

---

[*] The *benti:* a hymn of supplication by Soami Ji Maharaj.

ward we then learn to use the other leg which is *dhyan* (contemplation) and with the use of these two we can walk firmly onto the ladder of the Sound Current and climb to the ultimate heights of Sach Khand.

On returning from satsang we were taken directly to have an audience *(darshan)* with the Master in his garden. He asked about our flight and then said he felt ashamed he had not visited England to see us rather than cause us to make the long journey out to India, but he had thought that, as the Indians had not seen their families for a long time, it would be better for them to come home. Diwan Sahib Daryai Lal, standing behind the Master, added very quietly, "And though it has been such a troublesome journey for you, yet, if you consider, Maharaj Ji has had to come down from Sach Khand to see you!"

Mr Schidlo, an American satsangi, said he thought that if Maharaj Ji were to visit England, many Americans would take the opportunity to come over to the United Kingdom to pay their respects. The Master said, "We shall see."

During the course of the afternoon we were taken on a tour of the *langar* (community kitchen) by Mr Khanna, who was our mentor. While we were being shown the great cauldrons of cooking food, he told us a very moving story. On one occasion some ingredient for *parshad* (blessed food) was in short supply and the new stock had not arrived. The *sevadar** in charge of that particular duty suggested that

---

* *Sevadar:* one who does seva, or selfless service, with no thought of material recompense.

Maharaj Ji should please consider giving out a little less than the customary handful to each person. When the distribution was made, Maharaj Ji gave a *double* handful, instead, to each satsangi and not only was there enough, but to spare, for everyone. Maharaj Ji then turned to the sevadar and said, "Please forgive me. I hope I did not do wrong!"

On another occasion he said to Mr Khanna, "I am the servant of the sangat—what they require of me, that I do." Mr Khanna said that all he could do was to bow at his feet, overwhelmed by his humility.

Tomorrow is the bhandara and one hundred twenty-five thousand are expected: eighty buses and four hundred *tongas* (horse-drawn cabs) as transport; some of the people will have walked two hundred miles to attend.

Soul Growth

29th December

Today we attended the big satsang at which there were about ninety thousand present. The congregation sang hymns as is customary before each satsang and then a man with a superb voice who had sung before the last two discourses gave a hymn of his own composition and, as he had done on former occasions, one of Kabir's shabds. He sang with all the feeling he could muster and with most fervent gestures. He had great histrionic power and a magnificent voice with deep conviction behind it. Though most of us did not understand the language, we could quite easily follow what he was saying.

It is customary at all satsangs for the Master to be attended by two *pathis* (chanters) who sit beside him on the dais. They sing in unison couplets from sacred poems written by previous Masters recognized as being of the highest order—those who have inculcated the Sound Current in their teachings as being the main means, through the instructions of a living Master, of finding our way back to Sach Khand, the home of the spirit. After the chanting of each set of couplets, the Master discourses on the subject, expanding its implication and drawing on parallels to underline its message. Satsangs are simple and straightforward with the minimum of ceremony, in the idiom which simple countryfolk can understand, for they form the bulk of the Master's audience.

Some of the satsang I understood as follows:

When you look at a tree, you realize it has sprung from a tiny seed (and here the Master gestured with his beautiful and expressive hands to show its smallness) and the little plant has grown slowly, slowly into a shady and spreading giant of a tree, which if you consider it, was all wrapped up in that small seed-case waiting to be developed; but if you had been told beforehand that this little seed would develop into such a gigantic tree, you would never have believed it possible. In a like manner, the soul and the Word are wrapped up within the body and mind of man, waiting to be developed by a true Guru.

He gave a vivid description of the descent of the soul from Sat Nam, first being caught in the lure of the mind and its handmaid, Maya, which by means of the senses, behaving like a courtesan, drew it away from its true bright destiny, at first by beauty in diversity and then, when this fragmentation was well advanced, by the blindness of ignorance and separation until pain and bewilderment filled its days. It no longer had any knowledge of its origins by which to set its standards; and, deluded by the tawdry alternatives offered by its new companions, it became bound down by the chain of action and reaction which, moment by moment, grew longer and stronger.

Instead of going within itself, he explained, it now grows an ego and runs outward to possess all it sees around it, only tying itself tighter to its terrible surroundings when all the while salvation is nearer to it than its own hands and feet.

This ego, he continued, is the chief barrier we have to any chance of a return to our true surroundings. It finds expression in such language as 'my, my', 'I, I', 'I like this, I hate that', 'my wife, my children, my property'. With this ego uppermost, we can never truly possess any of these things nor attain the permanent happiness with which their possession seems ever to lure us. This can only be achieved when 'I' and 'my' are shed forever.

Sometimes the soul becomes dimly aware of its predicament and tries to purify and redeem itself by living the life of an anchorite or by practising one of the dead, hollow, outward religions of this world in temple or mosque.

"Literally our only hope is when in human form, we find a guide who knows the way out of this maze and learn the technique from him of withdrawing our attention to the third eye"—and here the Master gestured again with his gentle hand to a spot between the eyes—"where we will contact the pure music of the Audible Life Stream, the source of life it-self. We will slowly, by ardent and assiduous practice, learn to discriminate and begin to see, in some small measure, the path our Satguru is trying to show us. At first, due to the jangle of our worldly life, we cannot discern the full glory of the harmony within us; but it is there, just as surely as fire is latent in wood, which, on being rubbed in the correct man-ner, springs to life.

"The whole secret lies in devoting ourselves so whole-heartedly to our Master's instructions that we not only re-semble him whom we love, but literally become him!"

Yes, I thought, this is what is meant by *bhakti*—true de-votion. It is to love one's Master and all for which he stands, so devotedly and tenaciously that all intervening material forces are dissolved and one automatically merges in him. This, then, is *bhakti!* Sach Khand is here and only my will stands in the way. The worst foe becomes a friend, for, by understanding him, I understand the motivation of all and perceive the stillness and peace at the core of life. Seeing it, I cease to have need of 'I' and become 'thou' and 'him'.

But the trouble is, I thought, that I cannot hold this idea in my mind all the time. I will get up from here and the world will flood in and the glory of this thought will be dis-solved like sunlight in the little boy's jug. What can I do to keep it?

Scarcely had I thought this when the Master's voice again reached my consciousness: "Man himself is utterly helpless, like a feather blown by the wind and is only given a sense of direction when God smiles on him. We are all beggars at his door and only by continually begging can we obtain his grace and then in his compassion he will hear and give us all."

Only by continually exercising the spirit will I strengthen it, I thought. Like every other activity in this life, strength comes through practice.

At least two-and-a-half hours of bhajan a day, he has said on many occasions. It all comes back to the Master; only he can give me the tenacity of purpose, the bhakti to carry this out.

After satsang we again had the blessing of darshan for five or ten minutes as there was much for Maharaj Ji to do, with the vast crowds requiring his attention. Some of our members went again to see the food blessed in the langar. After lunch we were hurriedly summoned to watch seva being done by thousands of satsangis. We saw earth being carried from the inner dunes of the river and thrown into the huge ravine-like depressions that run down to its bed, in order that a road may be built from the guest house to complete a circuit of the Dera.

At first we stood on the outskirts of the throng but later Mohindar took us through to where Maharaj Ji was standing on a mound. A steady stream of sevadars bearing full baskets from the dig site was flowing past like a river of earth on one side and running back to the site with empty baskets on the other. All ranks and degrees were carrying the earth joyfully and singing, with adoring faces turned towards Maharaj Ji as they did so. At one moment they tried to get close to him, slowly and slowly, edging their path higher and higher up the hill until they were standing solidly around him and had to be put in motion again at a reasonable height.

Maharaj Ji spared time to talk to us and said it may take two years to complete the project, for seva could only be done with appreciable progress at the times of the big satsangs; but, he said, there was no need for hurry.

He agreed to our attendance at tomorrow's conferring of initiation on a large number of applicants, and permitted us to take photographs and to sit silently enjoying the great harmony of his darshan. He kept altering his position, looking at different groups quietly and with calm, loving eyes, which note everything. Today, with all those thousands at satsang, he told our 'shepherd', Mr Khanna: "One of your people is missing", and noticed who took photos and many other small happenings that the ordinary eye would easily miss. For a long time he watched two women with a baby, that one of them was nursing; this over, and the babe safely asleep, they confidently left it on a tiny ledge within Maharaj Ji's view to return to their seva, a most touching example of faith and trust.

No manpower is wasted during seva time. Taking care of everyone's shoes and extra clothing was an ancient blind woman, too feeble to traverse the rough terrain in safety. Another, an old grandad, was acting as a human 'keep left' sign between the people with full baskets and the empties. They carry shallow baskets made of rough wicker on their heads, their knobbly surfaces insulated from the head by a 'doughnut' made of rags, shaped like a deck tennis quoit.

One man seemed determined to pay off as much karma as he could in one effort and insisted on his basket being filled twice as full as any one else's, running with it full speed to the dump.

Yesterday we witnessed a perfect example of the Master's thoughtful grace. We had come back behind him through the Dera towards his house on our way to our quarters. When we reached the lane before his gateway, our own way through was blocked by an eager crowd waiting for darshan. I remember thinking to myself, How are we going to get through? Without a moment's hesitation he led us into the haven of his gateway for a few paces and then, turning, paused to bid us a graceful "Radha Soami!" giving us the breathing space we needed until the crowd had dispersed from the lane. It was so beautifully and kindly done and evoked our loving and silent thanks.

30th December

Today we witnessed the initiation instruction held in the big satsang hall which has a ground plan inside like the letter T, in the main stem of which sat the prospective candidates—all married couples, about four hundred and sixty pairs. Maharaj Ji sat in a chair before the dais area and they filed past him—those who were accepted going to the right wing of the T, and those rejected (only about five per cent this time) to the left and out of the hall. Each accepted candidate was given a card after they had been closely observed and briefly questioned by the Master. The accepted couples were divided, the women sitting on one side and men on the other. The Master then went out of the hall for a time, and the candidates were gathered closer around the dais, all the doors being locked and the upper galleries searched, for at initiations only satsangis may be present. The Master then came in again and in a very deep, quiet, kindly voice gave instructions along very similar lines to the present written directions given to overseas candidates by representatives abroad. When talking he uses his hands to perfection with a great economy of gesture; as they are such beautiful hands, each gesture is completely expressive—full of love, purity and beauty.

After the instructions were given, Maharaj Ji made the candidates repeat the names and regions five or six times each and then went outside again for a time. Sevadars were then deputized, and repetition of the names and regions continued to be taught for about fifteen minutes, when Maharaj Ji returned and completed the instruction of the Sound Current, explaining the position for simran and dhyan and the change for bhajan. We all took up the requisite position for bhajan and meditated for about twenty minutes in his blessed company. The candidates were asked what they had heard and Maharaj Ji gave a final speech of blessing. There were no further activities today as a second initiation took place in the evening after the Master had again gone down to be present at seva by the river, where a side road is being built in the form of a ramp from the main road. This will lead down to the river and be convenient for sevadars on their way to cut reeds for fuel and for cremations.

31st December
Again today there was no satsang, with darshan for the Western visitors only for a few minutes. At seva a top dressing of soil was put on yesterday's road.

A street of leasehold houses* for the use of resident satsangis is being built, consisting of one- and two-room suites.
Owners are asked to agree that others may occupy the accommodation in their temporary absence.

Captain Purshotam Singh (Shoti), the Master's brother,
took Mr and Mrs Schidlo and Ron for a drive to Baba Bakala,
a nearby village, this evening.

1ˢᵗ January, 1962

A beautiful satsang was given this morning, at which
Sardar Bahadur Jagat Singh's widow was present—a frail old
lady held in great respect by all.

During the course of his satsang, Maharaj Ji drew our
attention to the fact that in this life we not only languish under the ill effects of our bad karma, but we reap rewards for
past good actions as well. Sometimes they may take the form
of a charming disposition or good looks which attract people
to us. They may cause us to be born with a silver spoon in
our mouth, having property, wealth or temporal power. There
may even be so great an accumulation of good karma as to
entitle us to a protracted holiday in the allurements of a para-
dise in Trikuti, the highest heaven of the mind. All happiness
on these planes tantalizes us with its illusive impermanence,
for as soon as the effect of the good actions which caused it
are exhausted, we either change within ourselves and tire of
them, they cloy us with their sweetness or else they are with-

---

* All accommodation is owned by the RSSB Society and now given free
for the use of sevadars at the discretion of the Master. [Editor]

drawn, leaving us frustrated and embittered. In time, even their memory fades or is washed away by death.

We are therefore, said the Master, either C-class prisoners undergoing hard labour or A-class prisoners on remission for good conduct, but in either case, we are inescapably prisoners.

Someone approaching the path once said: "Why should we not seek to do good in this world, to improve conditions for the poor and follow a mission of relieving suffering? Surely this is a good attitude to adopt."

Here then was the Master's answer, for however we seek to improve world conditions we are only transforming C-class prisoners into A-class ones. We may be able to congratulate ourselves on the results, but have we stopped to consider how our own mind has been subconsciously and egotistically affected?

The only way one can help the world is to subdue one's own mind, said Maharaj Ji, and this may not be done by discipline alone. If one confines a viper in a basket, one only remains safe so long as the lid is shut (for the viper in the basket does not become a dove, just as a thorn bush nurtured in a vineyard does not bring forth grapes.*) Severe penances keep the mind under duress, but the first perfume of worldly allurement wafted past our nostrils immediately activates the very ego that we made such Herculean efforts to calm and extinguish.

In the satsang, Maharaj Ji went on to say: "It is only Nam or Shabd that effectively kills the ego. Nothing equals

---

* The Bible, *Luke* 6:44.

it for the purpose of 'knowing oneself' and attaining God-realization. Absolute, eternal and real truth is the Shabd and all other practices are inferior to it, for they keep us forever in delusion. Shabd alone pierces the dense clouds of maya and pulls us up into the great daylight of eternity. It takes us into reality and grants us ineffable peace and bliss."

Parshad was distributed after satsang to all, that of the Westerners being in little leaf cups skewered together with a twig. We had darshan afterwards, Maharaj Ji asking after the health of one sick member, commenting on the beauty and warmth of the day and asking for comparisons with our various countries—South Africa, Canada, America, Germany and England. He bade us welcome to a New Year party at his house this afternoon at 4:30 and gave us each a signed portrait as a New Year card.

Yesterday the Himalayas were obscured by clouds and today they have emerged capped with snow floating dream-like high above the plain. The air is unbelievably clear and the sky looks as though it had been washed. It is quite hot in the afternoon, though really cold as soon as the sun sets and until it gains power in the morning. Yesterday was dull and chilly.

We attended Maharaj Ji's New Year party, which was held in a marquee in the garden between his new house and Dr Johnson's *kothi* (house). Maharaj Ji and Harjit, his wife, bade us welcome at the entrance and a buffet meal was laid out on tables. We ate first, the food arrangements were excellent and the cooking superb—all Indian sweets and savouries. Later Harjit opened the entertainment accompanying another Indian lady, Bibi Ralli (who was an attendant in the household since Hazur Maharaj Sawan Singh Ji's time), singing and also playing a harmonium. Many Indians sang and recited and all the Americans present gave a rendering of the pre-satsang shabd they sing in the U.S.A. Dr Randolph Stone, an American satsangi, expressed the feelings of all Westerners when he said, in a short address, what a wonderful opportunity the people of this country had with Maharaj Ji, so to speak, on their doorstep, whilst we have to come thousands of miles to see him, an opportunity not all of us have even then.

While the party was in progress, a little owl flew in and around the tent, closer and closer above Maharaj Ji's head. He gave it a single look and, having accomplished its mission, it flew out into the night.

Rao Sahib Shiv Dhyan Singh (Harjit's father) and Sardar Balwant Singh (in charge of land and agriculture at the Dera) took part in a joint act in which they recited some English doggerel which brought the house down. Later Rao Sahib, that delightful old gentleman, with all the courtesy of a past age, said to Ron, "Pardon an old man's follies!" Otto, a young German satsangi, and Chacha Ji, a relative of the Master's, had an eating contest. Maharaj Ji, as always, was his most beautiful graceful self and yet enjoyed himself enormously. My husband presented him with two copies of the German translation of *The Inner Voice (Die Innere Stimme)*, which had been prepared in Europe, and an invitation to our next satsang in England, which caused some merriment. We also met Professor Janak Raj Puri, the brother of the author of *Mysticism—The Spiritual Path*.

Earlier we had watched *mitti seva* (earth-carrying service).

2*nd* January

An initiation instruction of the women took place in the satsang ghar, at which about ninety-nine per cent were accepted. We were bidden by the Master to accompany him into the sunshine on the verandah outside while the new initiates were being taught the names and regions by the sevadars. There were only about six of us this time. We sat for a time on the Master's cotton mat *(dhurrie)* whilst he reclined with his legs raised, seeming very tired. We all felt he ought to be alone but were reluctant to suggest it. There was an archway over our heads in which the wild bees had built their combs, and they were flying around us rather alarmingly. At first Maharaj Ji suggested that they would not harm us if we did not seek to drive them away—'bee flies' he called them! Some of us were still nervous, however, and so he kindly suggested we move away onto another dhurrie. This indirectly provided him with the rest and withdrawal we thought he should be having.

Later Margaret and I walked to the lone tree some distance up river from the Dera, under which Dr Johnson is said to have passed many hours in meditation when he was alive. We went over the sands and through the reeds by the river and up to the tree through one of the enormous clefts made in the clay soil by rivulets draining the surrounding higher countryside and running down into the river. We had a strenuous walk back—a miniature mountaineering expedition—by keeping further inland across the lie of the clefts which are in some cases thirty or forty feet deep.

Some of our number inadvertently got inveigled by an Indian satsangi into a thirty-mile car ride to Amritsar, and their absence caused some anxiety. It drew our attention to the fact that we were not supposed to leave the precincts of the Dera without Maharaj Ji's knowledge. Later, without any knowledge of their absence, he told us that we should always inform him of our intentions of going out anywhere as he is personally responsible to the Indian government for our safety.

3rd January

Today we had satsang with the Master quietly sitting whilst a pathi recited a shabd and gave the discourse. Maharaj Ji, beautiful and statuesque, sat there looking lovingly at us all, "full of grace and truth". We had the customary satsang for Westerners in his garden after that and a particularly good English translation of the bhandara discourse was read to us by Mr Khanna. I asked that a tape of it be given to the overseas satsangis and Maharaj Ji said he would try and make a synopsis of it for us, as it was very long. It was quite the most beautiful so far that I have heard, strong in parts but most moving and poetic.

Some good questions were then asked. Mrs Jepp, affectionately known as Jeppie, asked if a soul for some reason had to undergo rebirth in a lower form after having been a human being, would it have to go down to the bottom of the life cycle and begin again? Maharaj Ji said that this might not be necessary; souls were incarnated in bodies according to the karma of their past lives and the desires they had projected during these periods. If, asked Jeppie, one had not completed one's repayment of karma after initiation in this life and one had no desire to come back to this world, but was permitted to remain in one of the upper regions to work it out, would one create new karma whilst in these upper regions? The Master again replied in the negative and said one would be repaying one's karma by doing bhajan, and even though there is no other activity there, this would take longer than if expiated on earth.

5th *January*

The days are slipping by so quickly. In these last three days we have been allowed to do seva—all of us—carrying earth for the new road. It is wonderful how exhilarating this is, with Maharaj Ji's eyes on us. Mohindar explained that this type of seva was considered to be the quickest way of subduing the ego, for no matter how high one is on the social scale or in one's own estimation, the carrying of earth on one's head or the covering of one's person with dust as such work entails reduces one's sense of self-importance.

A little girl has 'adopted' Alex McCaskill and every day at seva she holds onto his hand and trots up and down with him, each of them with baskets on their heads, her basket a miniature edition of his. Her name is Savitri Devi and she is about six or seven years of age, a young woman of great firmness of character, who directs him to positions calculated to get a full basket most quickly and issues clear instructions as to just how much his basket is to be filled.

Great was my joy when told by the Master today that if my passport arrangements could be completed satisfactorily,

I might stay on for two or three months and that Ron would be cared for, going back alone.

At morning satsang for Westerners, Maharaj Ji spoke most inspiringly the other day. The conversation had become general and on a rather mundane level. We were talking of the crowded state of the Western world and Maharaj Ji slowly and very delicately turned the conversation round to more spiritual levels. He said that perhaps the only understanding the world could know could be brought about by a common language. He seemed to indicate that a particular nation's language might not be acceptable but an international tongue like Esperanto might meet the case, but then there seemed no impetus for nations to promote and to learn it. Only on spiritual levels could we become one big family. Look, he said, how all nations meet in Beas in an utterly friendly way like one large family with such mutual love!

A helpful question raised by Claud Lovelace was: "How should we answer people who casually enquired into our way of life and Sant Mat?" Maharaj Ji said we should not hurt people's religious susceptibilities. Sant Mat is not another religion to enter into competition with those already existing. Its way should be a positive one, not decrying other religions but being capable of standing on its own feet and appealing to people by giving them something outstandingly pure and sweet, so that they were attracted to it without any sense of comparison. The attraction then would be automatic.

During the conversation about nationalism, Maharaj Ji, spilling over with laughter, told us how he had brought a Siamese dress home for Harjit to wear. He described it as being long and straight, with a slit up the side and he said, "I suggested laughingly to her that she should wear it and just try it a little, but she said 'No!' She refused point blank."

At Harjit's invitation I had the honour of cooking Maharaj Ji's lunch, assisted very kindly by Jeppie. We were told he enjoyed his meal, especially the main course about which I had some trepidation.

When we came back from satsang behind him today to his own garden, I got a curious feeling whilst keeping my eyes on his person walking ahead. One had no sense of a personality trying to express itself whilst walking, as invariably happens, in one sense or another, with anyone else. There was such a sense of joy and grace, of quiet dignity, barely expressed by an outside body like a beautiful being enclosed in light, wearing his body lightly as it were, all of us following behind, going so lightly, I felt, and easily, as though we were treading air. Even when we fell behind a little or drew nearer to him, it was as though a spiritual thread of elastic attached each one of us to him and it stretched or shrank accommodatingly with the change of distance, making nonsense of any future parting from him in time or space.

6th January

I felt this same connection with him again this morning in another way. We had collected for his darshan in his garden early before setting forth on a day-long trip to Jandiala, Gurchetan's village. Only the British group was to go, English and Indian, at Maharaj Ji's behest. After bidding him good morning and asking for his blessing on our journey, we gave and each received a loving "Radha Soami" in his cherishing voice, which makes each one feel like a specially beloved child getting his blessing. Though leave-taking had been completed, we all stood around as though by common consent, saying nothing but very loathe to leave his dear presence. I said, "And now we feel we don't want to leave you!" We all laughed, the feeling was so spontaneously mutual and beyond human words in intercommunion.

The journey to the village was made in two cars, Maharaj Ji's jeep and a borrowed car. It was a 'day of the gods', as almost every day seems to be here, fair weather, clear, smiling and sunny. We were given a spontaneously joyful welcome at Jandiala and met, first of all, Gurchetan's sons and other relatives and the father of Mohan Singh, one of our other Indian satsangis in London (he resembled Mohan as he might be in years to come). They led us in a procession of villagers, simple and unaffected in their delightful welcome, to Gurchetan's house where we were met and the women amongst us were embraced by his handsome wife and daughter. We climbed to the rooftop, where, on its flat surface, we were regaled with a sumptuous Indian meal served on a long table under an awning with canvas screens around us, all colourfully patterned. Even so, an eager curious crowd of young women and children peered at us—quite inoffensively—from nearby roof tops. Shrieks of mirth and giggling broke out when we turned and noticed them and this precipitated flight when cameras were turned on them at first, but later photos were taken with much good humour and friendly chaffing.

The whole occasion was one of such open-hearted love and pleasure on both sides.

After lunch we were conducted around the village by eager crowds, children, dogs and poultry—all agog since they had not seen a white face for thirty years, but still with the same good humour and loving dignity as we felt the Queen might be given on a royal tour. Suddenly we were embraced in the street by a dear little person who turned out to be Mohan Singh's wife, a charming little lady who took us into her small but very clean house. We sat in rows on two beds and the whole village populace seemed to be pressing in at the door and filling the ante-room. She bade them open a side door for air, and the crowd was waiting courteously silent, but as eagerly at that entrance too. I got such a strong impression (and others felt it too) of a biblical scene—as when the room being too crowded, they let the man sick of the palsy down through the roof for Christ to see (but *our* Saviour was not with us in person this time!). In fact the rural simplicity and atmosphere all around was very reminiscent of scenes described in the Bible.

We went back for tea on the roof—another tastefully cooked and served meal, and met many people, some non-satsangis, all seemingly searching and ready; one Sikh gentleman, a retired Indian Army captain, appeared very near the truth. We had such a feeling of perhaps being 'path straighteners' and to our joy heard that Maharaj Ji intends holding satsang at the village on 29th January, later confirmed by his own lips to Gurchetan. Gurchetan is reported as having an-

swered the Master's enquiry as to when he was proposing to
go back to England by saying, "Not, Maharaj Ji, until your
honour deigns to visit my village!"

We again had a loving darshan of the Master on our return. He was interviewing other people on one of the house
lawns when we came and the siren went for evening bhajan
while we waited. We sat and did our simran, getting all the
benefit that such an environment created in us. When he came
to us, with gentle humility Maharaj Ji begged our pardon for
keeping us waiting. God's most perfect emissary on earth begging our pardon for *permitting* us to do simran in his house!

Dr Schmidt, an initiate of Maharaj Sawan Singh Ji, had
arrived by air from Switzerland whilst we were in Jandiala.

7ᵗʰ *January*

Dr Schmidt asked if I would help him type and translate his impressions of initiation. Maharaj Ji had apparently
recommended that I assist him in this capacity.

10ᵗʰ *January*

The last three days have been spent mainly in organiz-
ing the committee work for the British sangat. Mr Ahluwalia,
the Dera Secretary, formulated a very able solution which,
however, Maharaj Ji apparently did not consider entirely fit-
ting, so he is going to tell us his plans tomorrow. It is bound
to be a masterly concept and solve all our problems. Mr Ahluwalia read us some of his translation of a shabd by Maharaj
Sawan Singh from his book *Gurmat Sidhant* (now translated
and known as *Philosophy of the Masters*). It was so inspiring

that it made us immediately wish to sit in bhajan. We understand it is soon to be published along with an abridged edition
of *The Path of the Masters* and four other books. At one of
the morning sessions Maharaj Ji approved of our proposed
pamphlet on the introduction to vegetarian cookery for new
satsangis and seekers, and said we may reproduce it and print
leaflets of basic recipes as suggested in it.

From the way Mr Ahluwalia spoke of book production,
we realized with what careful discrimination they handle any
matter connected with printing. One can fully understand this
when one considers what a potent instrument for good or ill
the printed word can be. In the wrong hands it could lead
more surely than most other ways to the reduction of a living
philosophy to a dead religion. All manuscripts are therefore
meticulously referred to the Master for his approval before
going to press.

This morning after Western satsang Maharaj Ji gave us
his proposals for the running of the British sangat—spoken
spontaneously with no written notes! He began to outline
the constitution of the committee and its duties, and as
spokesman I took notes whilst listening and quickly made a
little 'tree' asking him to verify its structure. He was kind
enough to use it and to ask me to draw up a draft of what he
had told us, for use as an indication, no doubt, that we had
understood what he wished done and for Mr Ahluwalia's
guidance in typing a fair directive. He asked me if I were satisfied and said that I could express any opinion quite freely as
to its suitability. I said that in my humble opinion it was a
perfect arrangement which only he could have devised.

Mr Ahluwalia had previously told us that the Dera is contemplating printing, in three languages, a periodical like our Sant Mat magazine in the U.K., *Spiritual Link*, the layout of which they greatly admired.

It might be a good idea to make maps of (a) London and environs, showing the relative positions of local groups and (b) England, showing central and local groups. Maharaj Ji was very interested in the numerical strengths of groups and their relative contiguity, also the distances between provincial groups and London. He suggested the names of five out of six of the personnel of the main committee and all the British group, and two out of five of the Indian group, leaving the choice of the remainder to each president. He said small local committees should have one person as their head chosen by mutual consent between themselves. He laid great stress on the fact that all committee members should think of themselves equally as sevadars. All decisions should be taken to further the quality and quantity of the individual's bhajan only. Committees—British, Indian and local—were given wide powers of self-determination within their own scope. When holding satsang, Maharaj Ji said, people could read or sing shabds, ask or answer questions, read from recognized Sant Mat literature or give talks and discourses on aspects of Radha Soami, but group meditation was not permitted. Satsang could be held by as few as two people.

All seemed very content with the Master's proposals. In consultation with Bea Jauncey, Gurchetan, Mr Kareer and Ron, I prepared the directive and talked the draft over with Mr Ahluwalia afterwards. Again the next day, I also further consulted Maharaj Ji in a private session on points of doubt. At the open meeting Maharaj Ji had stressed that honest differences of opinion could be referred directly to him provided they were of an important enough nature. Where such differences affected the executive running of the sangat, however, presidents should be kept in the picture.

At the satsang immediately preceding the meeting I asked the Master to recapitulate one's method of collecting the attention at the third eye. He described how the nine doors should be closed and the attention taken upwards with a progressive loss of sensation from the feet upwards and a feeling of pull at the *tisra til*. Dr Schmidt asked if this were situated three inches behind the forehead in the pineal gland. Maharaj Ji responded that one could not tie it down to an exact anatomical position. It has a mental and spiritual existence and not a physical one. One should not try to imagine it being in a certain spot between the eyes, nor turn the physical eyes backward and inward in one's effort at concentration. If one concentrates on the spot mentally, finally one's limited consciousness will cease to exist and will then encompass the whole of creation.

Partings

11ᵗʰ January

Today was the sad day of departure for five of our number: Ron, Claud Lovelace, Alex McCaskill, May Holt and Jeppie. After the two morning satsangs, all departing ones are to be given time with the Master. They are to go on the 9:20 p.m. Frontier Mail (air-conditioned class) to Delhi, pick up their passports and tickets from Mahatta's photography shop which is owned by the Mehta brothers, have lunch there and fly at 6:45 p.m. to Bombay where they will catch the plane to Karachi and go home.

At satsang this morning Maharaj Ji drew a parallel from our recent experiences and said that when one buys an air ticket and obtains a passport, going through all the preliminary preparations for a journey, either by sea or by air, it is because one has faith in the pilot's or the captain's ability to arrive at his destination, never doubting that he will do so. In the same way one should make use of all the preliminary aids to spiritual progress such as simran, dhyan and bhajan to reach Sach Khand, knowing full well that one will succeed in one's purpose and that one's guide, the Master, will conduct one unerringly to one's destination. Studying a road or rail guide alone, however, cannot take us to our destination until, in the light of the information they contain, we prepare ourselves for the journey, buy the ticket and sit in the train or other conveyance. In a like manner, reading holy or inspiring books cannot achieve our object. Doing so is like cleaning a vessel but if the whole of life is spent in cleaning alone and nothing is put into its emptiness, it is a sheer waste of time. Our mind has, indeed, to be cleansed in order to fill it with the divine nectar; reading such books is better than not doing anything to seek salvation, but practice is infinitely superior, for it is this alone that 'delivers the goods' and leads to salvation.

"Intellectual gymnastics and argument", Maharaj Ji said, "create rather than demolish the walls that separate us from God. Through them you can rationalize your belief but never can you succeed in attaining salvation. In fact, the more we indulge in them, the further we recede from our goal."

The Master continued, saying that one can accept what one reads, like a sheep following its kind blindly, but it is only by actually sitting in sincere meditation for at least two-and-a-half hours daily that one gains the discrimination *(vivek)* to sort out the wheat from the chaff in not only what one reads, but in all daily contacts. It is only when we begin to relate even the smallest happenings in our daily life to the Sound Current and the Master that true enlightenment dawns on us and we see everything by that inner illumination, and then what contentment, pleasure and joy we begin to experience. All life begins to have a richness of meaning we never supposed possible.

"Without Nam", Maharaj Ji said, "the mind remains a wild horse that runs out of control at the slightest pretext or whim....We have to comprehend for all time that what matters is the bringing of one's body consciousness into the orbit of the divine melody."

One of the basic rules of Kal's domain[*] is this tendency to orbit—this in a physical or mental way is what all nature is doing. Physically we are drawn to, dazzled or fascinated by phenomena on this plane and our potentially wonderful mind

---

[*] Kal's domain: the physical, astral and causal planes, all below the realm of pure spirit.

becomes besotted by the physical senses, the points of contact with this physical universe. When it breaks away in death
or in religious transport, unless it has a perfect Master, it
continues to orbit around the allurements of the higher mind,
which in its turn only moves in a circle (albeit a larger one)
and so it is led inevitably back to rebirth on this plane. It is
incapable of realizing perfect spiritual repose but must forever restlessly spin in orbit around one obsession or another.
Having done so for so long, this is the only way it knows
how to behave. Therefore the Masters use this very habit by
training us to transfer our obsessive tendencies to a worthy
nucleus—a true Master who will gradually draw the soul out
of its bodily isolation. Eventually the soul realizes its true
nature, sheds the sheaths of mind and unites with all other
souls and with God.

When we arrived for Western satsang, we found the
Master laughing in high good humour, Louise Hilger, an
American disciple, having drawn his attention to a small ink
spot on his hand which she had noticed. He said, "The slightest thing out of the ordinary is noticed. One day I had a small
rent in my trouser leg and about twenty satsangis remarked
on it to me after satsang!" Someone asked him how many
ways there were of tying a turban and he said, "As many ways
as there are wearers—I only know one way", pointing to his
own. I said I supposed each way was characteristic of the
wearer like a thumb mark, and he said yes.

Annabella Blankenberg, another overseas visitor, caused
a good deal of amusement when given her parshad. She said
she had not known till recently that it was anything special

and had eaten hers at one sitting! The Master was very diverted by this and said, laughing, "No harm, no harm. The
sooner it is eaten the better!" The Indians are most careful
of their parshad and will meticulously pick up and eat the
smallest crumb even if it falls in thick dust.

All departing satsangis were given parshad and when
anyone offered to pay money into the langar, our gracious
Master smiled and gently told us that we had done enough
seva in coming here and paying our fare. "Besides," he said,
"you have done seva here also, I have seen you!" Each departing satsangi was also given a most expressive signed photograph of Maharaj Ji. This evening the guest house hummed
with the activity of departure. We saw them off at the station,
making two journeys in the jeep to do so. Some of the Indian
visitors are travelling back with them.

12th January

Today the Master leaves for Delhi to give satsang there.
Two of our number will be going with him by road, whilst
three more go by rail. We all went round to his house to
have darshan before he left; quite a small crowd had gathered
in his garden. The route in the Dera was thickly lined with
the remaining inhabitants. The car was filled to capacity and
the sun had not long risen—one of those glorious sunrises so
specially a part of the Dera landscape. Away they drove to be
stopped no doubt by satsangis at many places on the way—
level crossings and tiny hamlets as well as big cities.

Later we heard that our voyaging satsangis, knowing
that Maharaj Ji had promised to see them off at Delhi, had,

almost bodily, held the plane up until he arrived aboard to wish them "Godspeed". Non-passengers are not normally permitted beyond the waving base, but almost miraculously he managed to reach Delhi in time to have a few minutes with them and give them his blessings before they left.

Marking Time

21st January

Nothing of great note has happened whilst Maharaj Ji has been away. Yesterday a great dust storm blew up out of the south-west. The air was almost like smog and the sun was obscured. It is early for such a storm which usually comes in March when the *looh,* the hot seasonal wind from the desert, blows for three days at a time. Today it is like a day in England: flat grey skies, a high wind, pouring steadily with rain and very cold after quite a violent thunder storm this morning. A day or two back we had a sharp night frost and all the hedgerows and jungle plants were black and withered the following morning. Before he left, Maharaj Ji suggested the advisability of attending satsang, which continues to be held every morning by one of the older members of the resident community whilst he is away.

Looking back on the time when Maharaj Ji was here, I have remembered one or two incidents. Speaking one morning about our apparent lack of success in bhajan, about which one of our number had complained, he said, "It is not success which matters! Even if you fail, it is a sure indication that you are applying yourself. It is the Master's responsibility as to whether you have success or failure", and then with a look of ineffable love, he said, "Bring me your failures!"

A little incident which occurred on the last morning he was here illustrates the unconscious magnetism which flows from him. He was standing talking on the right-hand side of his car just before getting in. Suddenly he said, "No, I will get in the other side", and saying so went around to the left-hand side to get in. Quite unconsciously we bystanders had all grouped ourselves on the right side and, like a flock of birds wheeling together in the sky, without a moment's hesitation we all changed over to the left hand side of the car. I could not help smiling for we had not realized what we had done, but the sight of so many acting spontaneously had brought home his great personal attraction.

Jo Howard and I have had two hours of wonderful talk with Khanna Sahib—this seemingly in answer to an unspoken prayer in my mind. I have been in bed for the last two or three days with eye trouble and have missed satsang sorely. Instead we had two hours of almost direct contact with Maharaj Ji in English, a communion of great love. Khanna Sahib related to us the story of Colonel Berg from America—his coming to the path and his initiation—and many instances, some amusing, from his own rich personal association with the Master, of his abiding love and care for us all. It was a notable thing that in all the stories about himself and his family, the joke was against them, but in the two about other people the illustration was in their favour; such is the charity and humility of those nearest the Master.

The Master Returns

26th January

Yesterday Maharaj Ji came back and we had afternoon satsang in the little hall with Gurbachan Singh taking the discourse and Maharaj Ji sitting passively. He had come from Sirsa via Chandigarh, the Punjab's new capital since Lahore was included in Pakistan. They say it is very beautiful and with one of the finest of Europe's architects—Le Corbusier—as its designer, this is not to be wondered at.

This morning we went as usual to Maharaj Ji's house for our little satsang and at Bea's instigation I asked: "When we dream, is it ever possible to go up into higher regions rather than that our consciousness slips down into the body?"

"Yes", he said. "If one's love is great and one's thoughts are habitually turned towards the Master, then one has experiences on a higher plane; but this is not usual." Dreams are the result of suppressed subconscious experiences during the day. One should not encourage sleep, he said, at bhajan periods, but simran was a wonderful aid to sleep. Fifteen minutes of simran, done before retiring for the night, would promote deep, restful, dreamless sleep, and in addition, turn the mind towards bhajan in the early hours.

He asked if I had heard from Ron and when I said, "No, Maharaj Ji, I have not heard yet", with such an air of mischievous triumph and a twinkle in his eye he said, "I have heard!" This caused a laugh and I felt all anxiety dispelled (as I had had no letter since they left on the 11th).

27th January

This morning he asked how many of us were going to Indore (in central India) and as I have been ill whilst he was away I asked if it would be wise for me to undertake the journey. He said laughingly, "Are your eyes and health all that is worrying you?" When I said yes, and that I did not want to be a nuisance on the tour, he said, "Well, you need not worry about that. After all we have a doctor"—pointing to Dr Schmidt—"with us and you would have to be cared for anyway, whether in Indore or Beas. You had better come!" There is always such an air of gaiety and holiday about any contact with him and he enjoys things so wholeheartedly. When he laughs, the whole of him explodes into hearty merry gales of laughter.

It seems as though he wishes me to stay on and go back with Bea after the April bhandara. It is so beautifully inferred without a direct invitation but so as to leave no doubt in the mind.

28th January

In disagreements he encourages all to speak their surmises, inferences or knowledge of facts with the greatest sympathy and kindness—the greatest respect for others' views, but summing up the position with a firmness that leaves no doubt in the mind. One is made aware, without his specifically saying so, that irrespective of whoever is involved in these karmic experiences, one should never forget that their karma was taken over by the Master at the time of initiation.

Both the actor and the acted upon are, therefore, only moving within his will and we should not worry ourselves or allow the mind to be swayed by apparent negativities.

Our duty is to attend to the purity of our own thoughts and actions and not to worry about the lack of integrity or the inexplicable in others' actions or thoughts. In keeping the mind on bhajan and simran, these things assume their true value, their impermanence, their illusory importance. They should be looked on only as an object lesson, leaving no permanent effect on our judgement of the people involved. After all, we cannot see the whole picture, so how can we really draw valid conclusions; we are so wrapped up in the importance of pairs of opposites—honesty and dishonesty, selfishness and unselfishness, purity of motive and impurity of motive, which are, after all, only Kal's weapons to keep us obsessed with the play of things on this plane. We are all single-minded in one thing only: devotion to the Master. Therefore let us find the solution to our misgivings in the only positive way known to us—this same *Guru bhakti* (devotion to the Master).

29th *January*

Maharaj Ji gave us a pleasant hour's viewing of slides of his Far Eastern tour and of scenes in the Dera. We saw three packets of slides and there are about fifteen! He said that for scenic beauty, Japan and Thailand were the most remarkable.

Two pictures impressed me the most. One showed the truly biblical quality of mitti seva with the Master standing high on a mound above the Beas river with a massive cloud effect behind him and the crowds of drifting sevadars making a lively swirling multitude around and below him, rather like a Rembrandt drawing. The other one was of Harjit and her daughter garbed for the wedding of Maharaj Ji's sister, in the traditional dress of the state of Uttar Pradesh—her own birthplace: the massive nose ornaments, the jewellery and full-skirted dresses, the brilliant fearless colouring of the Rajputnis together with their queenly deportment.

Transport

31st January

Today has been an unforgettable experience in this period of memorable events for we have travelled to Delhi for seven hours with God's divine emissary! This sounds perhaps like an over-emphasis, but I have never had such a transport of unworldly travel! There he was in person travelling beside us, but the material presence seemed of a fineness, a lightness, a fragrance that divested our trip of any resemblance to ordinary journeying. We left at 9 a.m. and I sat witness at the receiving end, so to speak, of the parting adoration of the Dera populace. Shining morning faces lined the route from his own back garden out through the precincts and to the entrance gate, all thoughtfully on the right-hand side of the car (the side he is known to prefer in travel). It was as though corn were bowing before the wheels of the car in its passage, but instead of swaying away from it, the people were bowing towards it with a long continuous murmur of soft

"Radha Soami" as we went. To some the Master inclined his head in return, some received just a loving look and to some he raised a hand. Sometimes the humblest attracted the warmest blessing, with that soft caressing voice repeating, over and over again, the most beautiful greeting in the world. The moments were full of indescribable shimmering love and wistfulness.

As we were crossing the bridge over the river Beas, one of us remarked on the drop into the river: "Many people committed suicide from here when Maharaj Sawan Singh died, did they not? Their love must have been very great, if misguided. How does this action rank in the court of the Lord?"

Maharaj Ji said, "Their action, of course, is not basically right and must be discouraged, but much will be forgiven because their love was great. Life itself became insupportable in the absence of their beloved Master."

Someone then said, "What a great thing love is. It truly knows no laws."

There was a moment's silence and then our Satguru said: "Give them love and there is no end to what they can do. Absolutely no end!" I thought, how true. That is the core of this philosophy. Where love is present, it breaks even its own rules. Where love is present, people as such do not exist, only a common purpose so impelling it knows no limitations and no one can resist its magic, its enchantment. They unite, purged of self-consciousness, aware only of the glory of the Guru and the stream of white music electrifying their beings and carrying them upwards to infinity. One sees this happening all around one, very unobtrusively, very quietly, all the time in Beas.

In the morning period we talked quite freely of this and that, and then Maharaj Ji gave us a revealing glimpse of family life as it has been customarily observed in India for hundreds of years, and of his family experiences in particular. He spoke of the habitual respect of the younger members for the older, the unswerving obedience, no matter what the inner conviction as to the fitness or otherwise of family happenings, to the family head, be it grandfather, father or in the absence of male members, grandmother, mother, etc. His own betrothal to his wife, for instance, was contracted by his grandfather (Maharaj Sawan Singh) without reference to his father and when announced by him to his father, the latter took it as quite the ordinary acceptable thing.

Also he pointed out the importance of the husband's mother in family life. The wife's mother hasn't the same authority in the family. In fact she very often sides with the husband in disagreements so as to ensure her daughter's happiness. Regardless of her own private conviction, the wife (sometimes, no doubt, with cajolery from her husband) inevitably obeys the will of her mother-in-law.

This way the sense of frustration and uselessness with which we Westerners are all too tragically familiar in our elderly relatives, is practically non-existent and they live a fruitful life, honoured and obeyed to the end of their days and of use to their community. He pointed out that this helps to banish worry from the younger minds too, the responsibility for any decision resting on the older, more experienced shoulders without question. When, for instance, he himself was due to go to college, he went to Maharaj Sawan Singh, who talked over his preferences with him, and then gave his irrefutable decision on his curriculum. If presents were brought for the family, as they were after his Far Eastern tour, they were all given to his own mother who decided on the suitability of each item for its recipient, without question.

He talked most lovingly of his own father and his complete and selfless devotion and generosity to his children. Once when Maharaj Ji's household larder had run short of flour at short notice, guests had arrived unexpectedly, so they had sent out to the nearest market for some flour as an emergency—his father's long established custom being to keep them regularly supplied from the family farm at Sirsa. Sardar Harbans Singh, his father, came unexpectedly on the scene and seeing the unfamiliar look of the bags asked from where they had come, and great was his indignation and distress when he was told. He insisted on the flour being returned to its source, and he sent off post-haste for his own supply.

He spoke of the family gatherings in his bedroom night and morning when the children came habitually to pay their respects and receive the affection of the parents. "Sometimes", Maharaj Ji said ruefully, "this is the only time in the day when I see them." This attitude of habitual respect becomes so established that it is passed down through the family automatically; when young, each is the recipient of love and the giver of obedience, and later the recipient of obedience and the receiver and giver of love.

He mentioned an occasion when his brother Shoti's daughter had, after consultation with their father, been sent to Sanawar school in the hills. A few months passed, Shoti having paid the first term's fee, when their father said to Maharaj Ji, "Charan, who is paying her school fees?" When told, he was quite indignant that they had not realized he would undertake this responsibility.

Maharaj Ji said, "Even when I was earning quite a good income as an advocate, my father used to give my wife presents of money quite frequently."

When we arrived in Delhi, there was an enchanting and spontaneous demonstration of fatherly love as a sequel to this conversation. Maharaj Ji had already lovingly embraced his daughter on arrival and they were both standing, talking of family news near me when he again embraced her, talking to her in terms of endearment and he turned up her face to his and kissed her very lovingly.

To return to our journey, when we arrived at Phagwara, Maharaj Ji gave us some nuts intended, so he said, for his children; then with such warm affection he looked around at us, which made me say "Well, are we not your children?"

We had lunch with the Superintendent of Police, Ambala District, and his wife, sister-in-law and child; such a nice, friendly, pleasant family. The meal was lovingly prepared and most tasty. The rice in India has such a noticeable fragrance when brought into the room, hot and freshly cooked.

Maharaj Ji stayed on a little while afterwards, going off later to pay other calls in the neighbourhood. We met him

again at three o'clock near the Ambala Club and continued
our journey. He likes to be silent for a while after lunch and
sat quietly amongst us, just looking at the countryside as it
passed by. His presence is so gentle as, at the same time, to
give the impression of not being there and being super-present
at once. I remembered Mr Khanna's description: "However
much one may strike a Master, nothing but milk and honey,
milk and honey flows forth!"

After about an hour we began to talk softly to him. Someone earlier on at the Dera had given the impression that the
Master had implied one should not make too much of one's
determination under all circumstances not to eat forbidden
food. If, they said, one found that a meal had been specially
prepared and contained products we should not have, one
might eat it in order not to give offence. I put this point to
Maharaj Ji and he was quite emphatic in his insistence: "No
compromise!" he said. "You have got a brain, you should use
it and refuse in such a way as not to offend."

Dr Schmidt made the Master shout with laughter by
adding quite solemnly, "No, no compromise. It is like kiss-
ing; one kiss, two kisses and before you know where you are,
there are twins!"

"What a sweet way you have of putting things!" exclaimed
the Master, laughing hugely.

"No", the Master continued. "If you refuse, even though
the company may tease you, they will respect your integrity.
Once, when I was still a young man, before I married, a family
with whom I was friendly asked me over for a meal and I

quite forgot to tell them that I was a vegetarian. They prepared a vast and sumptuous meal with many dishes, all containing meat. I excused myself, whilst feeling very upset that I could not do justice to their hospitality, but confined my meal to curd and chapatis. They teased me and laughed at my meagre diet, but that family is now all satsangis!"

Dr Schmidt asked: "If one takes pleasure in eating and the careful preparation and enjoyment of food, is this a bad thing?"

"In itself it is not bad, provided it does not disturb bhajan in any of its aspects."

Another small incident occurred during the journey which caused us to ponder. We had stopped to replenish the car with petrol and a man offered us bananas for sale through the window. Maharaj Ji said, "Would you like some bananas? I cannot have them but if I could, these look very tempting." Then after a minute's pause and with a small smile he said, "The temptation has passed." (He is on a very low starch and sugar diet as his blood sugar has a tendency to rise easily.)

1st February

Maharaj Ji is staying in Delhi with his father-in-law, Rao Sahib. Bea, Dr Schmidt and I are with Mrs Sheila Bharat Ram, whose husband is a prominent industrialist in this country. Her home is as elegant as her heart is large and hospitable; she never spared herself where our comfort and entertainment were concerned.

2nd February

Yesterday we had a pleasant evening as Sheila arranged a dinner party, and to our great pleasure Maharaj Ji had time to attend together with Harjit, their son Cuckoo and daughter Nimmi, Harjit's two brothers, one of whom was our old friend Rajendra. Other guests included Jo Howard from South Africa, Lemoni Ziller from Canada, Margaret Benson-Cooke, Mrs Lalri Shahani and Dr Chand, besides the existing house party, and one of the younger Mahattas, who brought a film of the Dera to show us. This proved most interesting from many aspects as it was taken in colour in Burreh Maharaj Ji's time *(burreh* literally means 'great' Master, and is the affectionate term used by the sangat to refer to Maharaj Sawan Singh). It was a record, amongst other scenes, of Maharaj Charan Singh's marriage in about 1944. Maharaj Ji was quite surprised, never having seen it himself. Harjit, a very young and bashful bride, appeared in it and a young, tall, slim, black-bearded Charan Singh in all the glory of a bridegroom's outfit with flower chains suspended from his turban. There was a lovely scene when there was an exchange of garlands between bride and groom, when the former was unveiled for the first time and she stood there, a very shy, girlish figure with modest, downcast eyes. At one moment her shyness completely overcame her and she hid her eyes with her hand and shook with laughter. Watching the picture, her children were doubled up with mirth and she joined in the common merriment. Maharaj Ji said, "Now Mummy is getting angry!" which increased our laughter.

3rd February

Next morning we were all packed up and started for the airport at half-past six to catch the plane to Indore at the Safdarjang airport, a small one suitable for inland traffic. We were due to leave at a quarter to seven, but owing to fog our take-off was delayed until after nine o'clock. There were many people to see Maharaj Ji away, amongst them his family and Mohindar. A satsangi pilot, Vishwanath, was flying the plane and another satsangi was duty officer at the airport that morning, both charming men. Finally we were airborne and Dr Schmidt got his wish to go up forward and inspect the flight deck with the pilot at the controls. The journey was uneventful with touchdowns at Gwalior and Bhopal before finally landing at Indore many hours later. We were joined on the plane in Bhopal by our host, Mr Sethi's eldest son, who flew with us to Indore where we were met by many more satsangis of the Sethi family, who garlanded us and drove us to stay at their joint family estate. There are three large adjoining mansions, one of which is a guest house built in the western 1930s tradition, all well-appointed, in which suites of rooms had been put at our disposal. We also met our delightful younger hostess, Shanti Sethi—who takes care of our meals in the guest house where Maharaj Ji and his immediate staff are staying. We are lodged in the care of another branch of the family.

4th February

About a dozen sit together with Maharaj Ji for all meals, except for breakfast which he has in his quarters. Each sumptuous repast awaits us in a dining room rich with colour, flowers and white damask napiery, little red place mats and red chairs. The food is lovingly cooked and served by the ladies of the family who account this a great seva. Satsang is held from five o'clock to half-past six every evening, with darshan in the morning. The attendance at satsangs has been anything from ten to twenty-five thousand, many coming from outlying districts; there are about six thousand satsangis in Indore itself. We had the privilege of attending initiation in three sessions, the candidates being some twelve hundred in number.

Before that, a day was spent sightseeing, first at Ujjain where there is a historical observatory called Jantar Mantar, said to be the oldest in India and supposedly situated on the longitude running down the middle of India at its junction with the Tropic of Cancer. According to the map this is not strictly true but it is poetic to believe so! The present observatory was built about the eighteenth century but the original one was built in Vikramaditya's reign (an emperor of the Maurya dynasty who lived some two thousand years ago) and its site is not known.

From there we went to see the Maha Kal temple, with which none of us were impressed. The worship was of Shiva— the destroyer—but the emphasis seemed to be paradoxically on his procreative aspect and one had to descend down, down, below ground level to the holy of holies—wet, dirty and *very* repulsive. What is more, we had to take off our shoes to go in and our feet were all mired up by the time we came out. Later I told Maharaj Ji of our experiences and asked why we should have had to undergo this strange karma. He said: "If you do not experience the darkness, you cannot fully appreciate the light!"

Next we went to see the palace of the Maharaja of Gwalior called Kalideh. It is an old Moghul building with the remains of what must once have been a beautiful water garden, but which was falling into disrepair for lack of royal funds. That evening we went to see the Jain Glass Temple in Indore built by the father of our host, Hira Lal.

During the course of one of his satsangs the other day Maharaj Ji spoke at some length on the subject of satsang. He defined it in Maharaj Sawan Singh's words and then expanded the theme:

Satsang—the discourses of the *gurmukhs* (fully evolved saints)—is like a fence around a crop. Just as the fence protects a crop against damage and loss, so does satsang afford protection and help to preserve the fruit of meditation for us. It enables us to digest and assimilate all the grace that is showered upon us. It is an insurance against the dissipation of that grace. Satsang, however, consists of sermons in which *only* Shabd or Nam is eulogized, in which the eminence of *gurmukhs* (the Masters) as Shabd incarnate is brought home, and through which emphasis is laid on devotion to Nam or Shabd.

That word *only* and the other injunction concerning gurmukhs stood out in relation to the Master's previous instructions to us (January 10) on the subject of conducting satsang in our own countries. It is a direction both to those conducting satsang and those passively participating. Every item, then, should be planned in the light of this direction and shown to be subsidiary to the axioms of Sant Mat, inspired by and firmly linked with them. The tempting digressions of the mind engendered by an emotional or nostalgic appeal only lead us away from our true destination; we are exchanging the part for the whole. In addition, the introduction of material not shown to be directly connected with the basic teachings of true Masters might confuse newcomers to the satsangs, seeking to know their pure teachings. These digressions might prove so insidious, so innocent-seeming, that the unwary might adopt them almost without realizing that rubies and gold are being exchanged for tinsel and glass.

Maharaj Ji went on to say that we should attend satsang frequently. "A stone which remains in water keeps cool although the water does not penetrate it; even then it is better than the stones outside the water. Likewise, worldly people come to satsang and are not affected by it, but this does not greatly matter. Anyway, they are better than the people who are so immersed in the world that they do not come at all. In course of time they will begin to accept its influence."

At first little or nothing may be absorbed but, as the effects of bhajan begin to be felt, satsang becomes significant and acts as an incentive to bhajan and vice versa.

When, as often happens with us in the West, satsang is not being held by the Satguru in person, one should not absent oneself because the delivery of the person conducting the satsang does not attract one. All satsangs held in the Master's name and according to his teachings, by whomever they are conducted, emanate in reality from the Master himself, however uninspired they leave us. They are, in fact, being delivered by the Master himself, who is using the person conducting them as his mouthpiece.

He continued saying: "It is the nature of the mind to be open to all sorts of doubts, but if one keeps in satsang and reads Sant Mat literature, those doubts or difficulties are automatically cleared and one feels impelled to work on the spiritual path."

Interest in Nam is only aroused by constant contact with the Master in every possible way. We should not allow outside interests continually to deflect us from attending satsang. This point was illustrated by a very apt parable: A blind man was thrown into a large prison which had only one door. He began groping his way, feeling the walls with his hands, hoping, in this way, to find the door and get out. When, however, he came fairly close to the door, he felt the urge to scratch his head, and in doing so he missed the door. In consequence he had to go round all the four walls again to find the door, but again he missed it for the same reason. We are in a similar plight and miss the only door which leads out of this prison of existence owing to indulging in pleasures and sense enjoyments, and have again to go through the whole cycle of births and deaths.

Every means of egress from this prison must be sought, for the mind will seek to hold us here; it is its nature to do so.

5th February

Most of the party went sightseeing to Mandu, a Moghul city about sixty miles away. Sheila Bharat Ram and I did not accompany them as we wanted to attend the initiation and be with Maharaj Ji. Also I was making a portrait of Sheila which we were anxious to finish. There were three initiations—two for men only and one for women only—mostly country folk, very simple and mainly vegetarians from birth. Their beautiful, transparently simple faces were a joy to look upon. They are Malvas, a Rajput tribe very similar to the people around Delhi. The men wore turbans, brilliantly coloured, white cotton jackets and loincloths *(dhotis)*. The women wore very full, calf-length cotton print skirts in daring combinations of colours, which, in conjunction with their golden-brown skin, black shining hair and lustrous brown eyes, always looked graceful and befitting. They wore long draped head cloths and little cotton waistcoats both in contrasting shades to the skirts, and jewellery—nose studs, chains and baubles around their ears and head, and anklets and toe rings of silver with little bells and chains on them which jingled as they walked.

You can imagine then the beauty of the scene when the women were waiting for initiation. (Maharaj Ji says that, as a general rule, women progress more quickly than men in the earlier stages and certainly the overall impression was one of more transparent unquestioning simplicity on looking at their gentle, shy, upturned gazes.) Row upon brilliant row of them, about six hundred and fifty at a time, were seated patiently waiting for him to arrive.

A curiously happy little incident took place the morning the women were to be initiated. For obvious reasons, a certain amount of care has to be exercised so that those rejected are excluded from the actual initiation. They sat, therefore, in the open in an alleyway between the orange trees of a walled garden with a small brightly coloured awning just over Maharaj Ji's position and a mat underfoot. The morning was one of sunshine and clouds and just before he arrived there was quite a sharp shower and we few initiates, permitted to witness the initiation, ran under the awning for protection. The candidates started to get a little restless when the rain showed no signs of abating; and as there was no room for them all under the awning, the situation was one requiring quick sympathetic thought. One of the women sevadars was equal to the occasion, however, and said, "If you stay still now, and suffer the storm to pass without moving, you will gain merit from Maharaj Ji." And she began to sing a little shabd in which they gaily joined, containing an allusion to rain:

> The season of rain has come,
> My heart is full of joy,
> My body and soul yearn for the Master,
> But the Master is gone abroad,
> If he return not, I shall die pining for him.
> The lightning strikes terror in my heart,
> I stand all alone in my courtyard,
> In solitude and sorrow.
> Oh mother of mine, I stand on the brink of death,
> Without the Lord I have no hunger, no sleep...
> Spake the Guru: She alone is the true wife,
> Who loses herself in the Lord.
>
> Guru Nanak, *Adi Granth,* p. 1108

They covered themselves with their shawls and presently the rain grew less and Maharaj Ji arrived. He had scarcely
seated himself when, as if by magic, the rain ceased and the
sun burst forth dramatically as our Satguru paused for a silent
moment's bhajan before commencing the instructions.

There were, in all, very few refusals, I should say ninety-
nine per cent acceptances. Though because of the pressure of
time and numbers the pace of interviews was fast, Maharaj
Ji's deep interest in each person's reply to his questioning
never altered or slackened: "You don't eat meat?" or "What is
the name of your village?" or "You won't eat meat any more?"
or "How long has it been since you gave up eating meat?"
He gave a little backward waving gesture of the head if they
were accepted; and said "Go, child, and listen to more satsangs" if they were rejected this time. The expressions before
and after were a most interesting guide to character—patient,
anxious, alert and expectant, or, "I'm not giving away my
feelings"; and afterwards, very devout and loving or rather
dazed; and if refused, also rather dazed, nervously smiling,
miserable or, "Well! It was worth a try"—in the case of the
very young who knew their chances were doubtful beforehand. Some argued with the assistants, begging for reconsid-
eration, but, all told, they were few in number.

Those who had been accepted were taken further away
to a walled courtyard covered with a marquee, the floor being
spread with cotton druggets (rugs), and the lovely initiation
instructions began.

As in all cases when there is a large gathering, loud-
speakers relayed the Master's voice. This seemed to puzzle

some of the more unsophisticated and although the Master was fully visible to all, one woman didn't know whether it was the Master or the loudspeaker who was conducting the bestowing of Nam. Her face expressed her bewilderment so transparently that we could not help smiling. Finally she settled for the loudspeaker and she nodded to it and smiled at the appropriate moments in clear sympathy with all it said. Bless her! She was probably far higher than any of us in her loving simplicity.

Whilst the Master spoke, I translated for Dr Schmidt and then the Indian women of the Sethi house party and I assisted in instructing them in the names. Many found them just as difficult to memorize as many Western folk do. One woman had mistaken the length of time one was supposed to do bhajan and assured Sheila that she would do her ten-and-a-half hours bhajan faithfully! We wondered what her husband would say!

15th February

After leaving Indore we flew back to Delhi and the party divided, Maharaj Ji going to his father-in-law Rao Sahib's house, whilst we stayed for a few more days with various Indian satsangi families amidst most loving and open-hearted hospitality. So complete was their sense of responsibility towards us that we were not even permitted to buy a stamp for our mail. Subsequently Dr Schmidt, Margaret Benson-Cooke and I spent about a week at Maharaj Ji's farm at Sikandarpur, Sirsa. It is a large, old-fashioned, solidly built house with farm buildings clustered around two large courtyards about a mile from the Hissar-Sirsa highroad with the village of Sikandarpur right against its walls. On the highroad itself is their sugar factory where the sugar cane is brought for crushing and undergoes the various processes to produce sugar and its by-products. Shoti, the Master's brother, lives here, manages the farm and is host to all the visitors who come during the season.

During our stay we had many long walks, sometimes accompanying Maharaj Ji, and though we mostly had our meals with Shoti separately, one or two were with the Master. On one memorable occasion he came up and sat talking for an hour or two with us. Towards the end we asked questions:

"When thinking of the Master in dhyan, should one look at his whole form, or head and shoulders, or head only?" asked Dr Schmidt.

Maharaj Ji said, "On the head only and more especially at the eyes."

Dr Schmidt continued, "In hearing the Sound, we are told we will hear both the bell and the conch, the high bell sound, then the lower, and finally the low sound of the big bell, the conch and the drum in Trikuti. Are these sounds continuous or intermittent and throbbing as in nature?"

"They are rhythmic", answered Maharaj Ji.

"Does one hear the bell or the conch first?" asked Dr Schmidt.

"Though described as separate sounds they are a part of the same Sound."

Dr Schmidt continued: "One goes through the pitch and intensity of the current from high, intermittent, shaken and uncertain, through the various pitches of the same sound until it deepens and grows more certain though still throbbing as in the drum?"

"Yes, that describes it", said Maharaj Ji.

"After seeing the Radiant Form, if one continues to hold the form of the Master in love and does not experience any of the other experiences in Sahansdal Kanwal, etc., can this be looked on as a true experience?"

"Yes, in the case of some people who would find this journey distracting or did not wish for these experiences, the Master helps them by taking them through without vision of the region."

"In the case of seeing the stars, the sun and the moon (given in that order in our literature), this seems against nature, if one were to be projected into space. Is that the correct order in which one sees these lights?"

"Yes, they are only words to describe the quality of the lights seen. One goes in, at first seeing only flashing light and very intermittently. Then this stills to a great extent and assumes rays as we imagine the stars to emit. Then the light becomes more golden in quality like sunlight and assumes the shape of a disc or halo. Then it softens and steadies and grows more silver resembling the moon in brilliance and shape. In each case you go towards it and seem to pass through it to get beyond it."

18th February

At meals Shoti told us many stories of their life and propounded novel points of view. It is as though in him Maharaj Ji had deliberately centred the extrovert social aspect of their wonderful hospitality. He entertained us for two hours hilariously without pause one evening with his experiences whilst on a tour of Soviet Russia, and one could see how no one was proof against his great good humour and personal magnetism, but it is so apparent that he carries a consciousness of the Master everywhere with him. "Emulate the honey bee" was his motto. "Sit on the edge of the honey jar tasting of its sweetness but do not fall in!" There was a deep personal bond between his grandfather, Burreh Maharaj Ji, and himself.

We have become better acquainted with Harjit and the three children since we have been here. The whole family seems instilled with vitality, good nature and a sort of glowing quality, which is hard to describe.

We left for two consecutive days of satsang to be held at Fazilka, a small town on the Pakistan border, chosen not for the largeness of its own populace, but because it is centrally located for the big satsangi membership spread about the local countryside. In the car with Maharaj Ji were Diwan Sahib Daryai Lal, one-time chief minister to a princely state and now Maharaj Ji's personal secretary; Chacha Ji, Maharaj Ji's uncle; Nimmi, his young daughter; Damodar, Maharaj Ji's driver, taking us there; and Chip herself feeling very humbly grateful, sitting next to Maharaj Ji. We sat pensively for the most part, being driven about a hundred miles to our destination.

21st February

We found we had been lodged to our great delight with Maharaj Ji at the Canal Rest House by the local sangat.

Mrs Usha Rajwade, with Bea as her guest, was to come from
Ferozepur, about fifty miles away, to attend the satsang and
I was to go back with her to stay for a time. We did not know
when she was to arrive and I expressed the hope that it would
be possible for me to stay for both satsangs and sleep the
night at the Canal Rest House. As though it was a foregone
conclusion, Maharaj Ji said, "Well, an extra bedding roll and
food has been brought, so you can stay."

I added, "If it is convenient for Usha", and he agreed.
Looking back on this conversation, I realize now how it set
the scene for what was to follow.

An officer, Colonel Ajaib Singh, serving under Briga-
dier Rajwade, Usha's husband, then arrived. He was not a
satsangi but had been a friend of Maharaj Ji before Maharaj
Sawan Singh's passing. He was greeted with open arms (and
hugged) by Maharaj Ji and sat with us in the sun for a time.
It was a most serene little bungalow in an attractive tree-filled
garden full of songbirds with a very pleasant atmosphere. Soon
the Ferozepur party arrived: Bea, Usha and an orderly along
with a satsangi family, Captain and Mrs Diwan and their two
sturdy little sons, all driven in Usha's elegant blue Mercedes—
much admired by Maharaj Ji—and we had lunch brought
from Sirsa by the Master. Shortly afterwards we left for satsang
and to our surprise the crowd was enormous, about seventy
thousand strong. The story goes that in Fazilka on normal
days it is rare to see a gathering of more than five people and
the like of this multitude had never been experienced before,
even when high political dignitaries had visited the place. All
the vendors and public transport people were taking full

advantage of the windfall and plying a brisk trade at the entrance to the satsang grounds.

Maharaj Ji, as is normal on these occasions, spoke over a microphone with a pathi singing the verses of the shabd in couplets upon which he expounded and enlarged. He usually starts speaking in a soft low voice, slowly warming to his theme, speaking for anything up to forty minutes at a time between couplets, almost uninterruptedly, and with no tricks of oratory whatsoever—a clear, firm, vital, straightforward delivery very occasionally emphasized by gestures when his beautiful, almost flower-like hands are used most eloquently.

Today he talked of the relative values of simran, dhyan and bhajan. Simran, he said, is the first approach to the Lord; it is the only 'work' that the Master has given us to do in order to reach him. It is a means of concentration. When we love anything in the world, we concentrate our whole attention upon it and think about it so much that we begin to identify ourselves with it—this is a form of love, earthly love. When our Satguru teaches us how to have spiritual love for God, he uses this same system of concentration. At first simran could seem meaningless but gradually, if we were to do it every day—at any and every time whilst doing our work or resting, whilst on journeys, the housewife in her kitchen or the man of the house doing his work—it would become automatic, running on subconsciously and then coming to the surface consciousness when we had a free mind again. We would then think: "Why am I saying these words? Oh! they are connected with the Master", and we would be drawn in thought towards Sant Mat.

Then, when eventually we sit for bhajan, half the work of concentration would have already been done and our mind would have been given its sense of Godwardness. We would then continue simran with our whole attention until we have shed the remaining pull of the world and absorbed all our thoughts into the third eye, one-pointing it like an arrow in its stiff streamlined purpose. It would then be ready to speed forth on its journey in a spiritual direction. At this moment we would see our Satguru in his Radiant Form—we ourselves having shed our physical body and all it stood for. We would be capable of seeing the astral beauty of the Radiant Master stripped of his physical form—a being of great attraction and light. The purpose of simran having been served, we would discard it and, holding the Master's form in our inner eye, we would begin to keep our attention on it with this newly acquired power of collected concentration. Now the Master at this stage is using the faculty of sight on the astral level to attract us, but his highest means of manifestation is Shabd, so, as we cultivate the habit of thinking towards this beautiful Being more and more, we begin to merge in it and become it, seeming to dissolve into it, transmuting the mere power of sight of his radiance into self-identification with him, and hearing his essence, which is Shabd. The form being no longer necessary, is left behind and all is Shabd—just as, when looking out of our own eyes, we are not aware of our form but feel the life-giving processes of our own body.

Therefore let us remember that our work is simran, simran all the time in our daily lives. He will do the rest if we concentrate on him through the words of remembrance.

The more we associate ourselves physically, mentally and then spiritually with the Master, in every one of his manifestations, the more 'fixed' will this habit become, and through being habitual, it will be a permanent and not just a haphazard association. We should not, however, allow ourselves to become self-satisfied and relax our guard on our ego, deluding ourselves into the belief that we have arrived. Such a conclusion could arise only through a temporary association, the ecstasy of a moment or elevation of spirit only during the bhajan hour or inspiration brought about by outside stimulation; for it is at these times when pride and ego seek to pull us down. We are only safe when spiritual identification with the Master is complete at all times; then, whatever we do will be karmaless—the Master himself will be the doer and not us.

After satsang, Usha said she would have to consider returning that night to Ferozepur as they had not come prepared to stay. One could sense, however, how all our thoughts were moving. I, for one, was miserably disappointed after the conversation earlier on with Maharaj Ji in which we talked of the possibility of my staying the night. There was a presence whose protection we were all loath to leave and an event the next day—his satsang—that we were all longing to attend. In desolation, Usha, wishing somehow to prolong the beloved hour, asked Nimmi if she would care to accompany us back to Ferozepur for the night, returning the next day with us. We could then attend the second satsang, to everyone's mutual delight. With Maharaj Ji's consent, Nimmi agreed and Usha accordingly went to phone her husband, but, as it had grown very late, he was averse to our travelling back at that hour, as the road was a very lonely one. I believe he guessed, too, Usha's desire, in common with us all, to stay at whatever physical inconvenience. So it was finally arranged that we could borrow bedding from the hospital doctor and his family, and buy fruit from the bazaar. There was plenty of accommodation at the Canal Rest House if Maharaj Ji would let us stay. So back we went, so many laughing bad pennies. Meanwhile at the rest house Maharaj Ji, looking around the empty rooms, had said to Diwan Sahib, "Too many beds and too few people."

On our arriving back again en masse, Diwan Sahib went in some trepidation to Maharaj Ji and said, "They have *all* come back!"

The Master remarked placidly, "That will be all right!" We did not think there would be food enough for us and were quite prepared to live off the fruit we had bought in the bazaar, but at dinner and breakfast the next morning there was more than enough cooked food for us all. Where did it all come from? Only a small canteen of food had been brought from Sirsa, approximately enough for the original party and we had already had lunch from it that day. There were five extra members and two children and there was still some left over when we had finished!

We had a most happy dormitory full of girls, and speaking personally, and I think the others would agree with me, we had a strangely restful night, in spite of a pack of pi-dogs with pups who seemed to be conducting a running battle most of the night between themselves and with stray jackals.

Maharaj Ji, in spite of being busy, seemed to be giving every opportunity possible for darshan and was in a gay, happy mood.

The theme of his satsang was bhakti—that higher mystic devotion for which we have no equivalent word and can only translate as the love of God. This was the shabd and the gist of what he said:

> In the court of the Lord,
> devotion and love alone count;
> devotion and love alone count,
> for devotion pleases the Lord.
> He declined a royal feast
> and took gruel with the son of a slave.
> They prayed and practised austerities,
> performed rituals of every kind,
> but he chose Shabri's berries,
> and the ascetics died of shame.
> Yudhishtra held a great ceremony,
> and all assembled there;
> pride that day died for all—without Supach,
> the bell would not ring.
> Paltu says, because of high birth,
> let no one feel proud;
> in the court of the Lord,
> devotion and love alone count.

This shabd, said our Master, is by Paltu Sahib, a saint whose incisive teachings give us a clear picture of the highest regions.

The love which we feel for God and which inspires all our actions consciously or unconsciously impels us to seek him, each in our own way. Some gather together in places of worship and others prefer the solitude of the anchorite in trying to look for him. Some think that good deeds will reveal him or that he may be found in books, but Paltu Sahib extols love as the only sure means of contacting him. But as He is invisible it is difficult to express a strong enough love to carry us into his presence. The sages of old found that in the five forms of creation—human beings, animals, birds, reptiles and fish, and plants—humans alone possess all five elements or *tattwas:* earth, water, fire, air and ether *(akash)*. A person could not therefore worship those forms of life lower than himself or he would find that by attraction he reincarnated into these forms at death. He could not worship his equal, his fellow human. Here he comes against a difficulty since there are no other tangible forms to worship.

At this point our great Master, Hazur Maharaj Ji, comes to our assistance with a very apt parable: "Imagine", said he, "a room full of unwired and disconnected radio sets. A technician would be needed to service them for us to get any news through them. We are in a similar position for we require the help of the great technician to link the radio within us—our soul—to our supply of power: the Sound Current, our source of life. Just as the radio waves are in the air all the time, but cannot be heard unaided by the human ear, so we cannot hear the Audible Life Stream resounding day and night within ourselves without the help of a perfect Guru— the only living being worthy of our devotion—who is, in the same breath, human and one with the All Highest. Through attraction for him we are drawn to the source whence he came and with which he is continually in contact. Only thus can we escape from the wheel of birth and death to which we are tied in the regions of the mind."

He explained the allusions in the poem thus:

When, during his travels, Lord Krishna was passing through the kingdom of the Kaurav prince Duryodhan (one of the principal characters of the Hindu epic *The Maha-bharat),* he did not visit the king as expected. Instead he preferred to visit the dwelling of Vidhur, the poor and lowly son of a serving maid who had no food to offer other than an unsavoury dish of boiled leaves with no condiments to relieve their monotony, but they had been prepared with loving care.

Paltu Sahib next referred to the story of Shabri, a poor tribal woman, low caste and poverty-stricken, who lived in the forest of Dandak into which the banished prince Ram Chandra (hero of another Hindu epic, *The Ramayan)* had wandered. There were many notable holy saints and sages *(rishis* and *munis)* who also dwelt in the forest glades but Ram thought to favour Shabri with his presence. Her larder was empty and she was reduced to collecting the only food her low caste permitted her to gather—the windfalls of wild fruit lying below the trees. To make certain that she garnered only the choicest of these, she tasted every one, in her desire to please her beloved guest, forgetting that the touch of her mouth meant ritual pollution of the food. Drawn by her love, the Lord came to her shelter and ate with great relish the meal she had so devotedly prepared, praising her for its delicious sweetness transferred to it by her loving care.

The third example given by Paltu Sahib, our beloved Master explained as follows: Towards the end of *The Mahabharat,* when the battle between the two rival branches of the ruling dynasty—the Kauravs and Pandavs—had ended in victory for the latter, they celebrated their triumph in the manner customary in those days with the ceremony known as *ashvamed yagya*. A horse owned by an overlord with surrounding vassal kingdoms was allowed to wander freely, accompanied by the king's champion. If detained by any princeling during its wanderings, this provoked war; but if not detained, the latter pledged himself anew to his overlord. Following this, a sumptuous feast was prepared and oblations were made in the presence of the local gentry and potentates.

On this occasion, Krishna warned them that the feast would not achieve its object unless the mystical bell sound was heard at its end. Not being successful, the Pandavs begged Krishna to advise them, from divine insight, how to remedy this state of affairs. He traced their failure to the absence of an anchorite, Supach, a low caste man. In their arrogance they believed he was unaware that free food was available nearby, and carelessly summoned him, sending an attendant to fetch him. To their surprise, he refused to come, even when the brothers themselves went in person to beg his presence. To their despair he stubbornly demanded the merit of, not one, but *one hundred and one* yagyas. The position appeared to be rapidly reaching a stalemate.

However, the gentle Queen Draupadi, taking a carefully prepared repast, went humbly on foot to the sage's retreat and implored him to relent, only to be given the same terms. She said meekly that these had already been obeyed, for was it not true that every step taken in loving trust towards an advanced soul merited a *yagya*? She had more than covered this requirement and begged that those steps over and above the requisite number might be held to her credit. Seeing her evident sincerity and clear piety, without a word he arose and accompanied her. At the conclusion of the feast, the bell's chiming was clearly audible to the overjoyed concourse.

These three instances, if carefully examined, the Master pointed out, reveal certain facts in common: neither worldly position, caste nor nationality (being in themselves trappings of this world) will ensure God's acceptance of our entrance into his realm. Only personal spiritual merit will enable us to start on the journey and only bhakti, or spiritual devotion, will prevail when we stand before his footstool.

This word *bhakti* is difficult indeed to render. In its beginnings it means at once the loving care put into any action, however small—any thought, word or contact by someone whose whole being is purified, strengthened and made sympathetic by simple living and a good karmic balance. Bhakti brings the soul, shining through its thin material covering, automatically into a natural cognizance of the Lord in the same manner as iron filings are drawn to a magnet.

Only an echo of this quality can be comprehended by our dulled understandings on this mortal plane for it requires a complete mutual understanding of one soul for another, which is almost incomprehensible to us, beset as we are by the limitations of our bodies and minds which separate us from each other and our source. None but a true saint can inspire such a love. One can go no further in words.

The Master followed this with another short discourse on a poem by Paltu Sahib, "An inverted well is there in the sky of the mind (Trikuti)":

> In the inverted well in the sky, a lamp is shining.
> A lamp is shining there without wick or oil;
> through six seasons and twelve months,
> it burns day and night.
> Only they who have found a true Master
> are able to see the light;
> without a perfect Master, no one can behold it.
> From within the lamp's light emanates a sound;
> it is heard by one in deep meditation—
> no one else can hear it.
> O Paltu, those who hear it,
> their destiny is fulfilled;
> in the inverted well in the sky, a lamp is shining.

Every action of ours in life whether mean or great, whether we realize it consciously or not, is a movement towards the possibility of realizing God—every ideal, every religion, every quest after happiness or peace—but how often do we succeed?

People seek for God on all sides but not within themselves, the only possible place where he may surely be found in his full power.

Only a fully awakened adept knows this and can give one the key—the Audible Life Stream—to eternal life and bliss.

Paltu Sahib, a saint who propounded this fact in the most fearless way, lived in the eighteenth century. He likens the head to an inverted well; when we first shut our eyes at the beginning stages of meditation, we see only its dark mystery within. In the guise of the body below the eyes, we go out into the world in order to live our lives in this physical world, but in the region above the eyes we seek our God. If by good chance we come in contact with a true Master, he will connect us with the current of the Word, the life-giving force within.

Paltu tells us that if we persevere with our meditation, having contacted such a Master, the darkness of the well will give way to the illumination of a light. Though till then we have been unaware of it, this brightness has really been there all the time, but our karmas have made us blind to its luminosity. It is of a spiritual and not a physical nature issuing as it does from Sahansdal Kanwal, which Paltu describes as the city of light, the first great reservoir of power which we meet on our inward journey. It is no mean achievement to have reached this stage. Saints and sages spent most of their very long and disciplined lives trying to deserve this privilege and it is only by the loving grace of our Satguru that our spirit has regained its power of perception. This, however, can only come about after complete surrender in devotion to him.

When we have completely withdrawn our consciousness from the body below the eye centre, there seems to issue from the light an entrancing bell-like melody. This inner sound is the real lost chord *(bani)*, but both Eastern and Western religious books understand it only in outward and strictly physical terms. It is obtainable only from a saint of the highest order. Many religious symbols are imitations of the realities within and were originally so used to encourage and remind us to seek their reality on higher planes. In almost any faith one cares to name, candles and bells have a deep significance. Hindus, Sikhs, Muslims and Christians all use them in one form or another. But alas, the purpose of the outward symbols has been lost and it has supplanted the inward reality. We can only find our way back when our accumulated karmas have reached an appropriate level for us to contact a saint from the highest region *(param sant)* who will take us back to those planes after re-linking us with the Audible Life Stream within.

The eloquent shining love of the satsang was the crown on this day when the Master gave himself so generously—to me, the highlight of my visit. The Indians were lyrical in their appreciation of it. With radiant eyes, Usha said, "He absolutely showered his grace, and there it was for anyone to take if they wished." Even the morning seemed to sparkle, a smiling beautiful day, with Sat Purush amongst his beloved multitude, not less than seventy thousand souls!

We came back after satsang to the canal bungalow where many people were waiting for darshan, having lunch later at the doctor's house and then returning to the canal bungalow. Here I had an experience that happened two or three times, whilst thinking wistfully of the Master. I was sitting on a settee alone in the lounge reflecting on all the events of the past two days and marvelling at the bountiful love we were witnessing, feeling also a growing sense of dismay at the thought of leaving his company so soon. I was looking downward and suddenly became aware of him in the middle of the room, almost as though he had manifested out of thin air, smiling so sweetly down at me, it quite took one's breath away. I said, "I was feeling a bit depressed at going away, Maharaj Ji."

With such gentle kindness he replied, "It will only be till the 28th."

A short while later, very reluctantly we took our leave of him. He was about to bless two sacks of parshad for distribution as we left and, to our minds, would be occupied some time afterwards before leaving on his return journey to Sirsa. We were driving out of the town talking quietly of him and recalling incidents with nostalgia when we saw his red car at a crossroads ahead. The time had been so short since taking our leave of him that none of us anticipated he would be in it. I said, "Look! Maharaj Ji's car!" thinking Damodar, his driver, was perhaps driving it to the town for refuelling. It still seems a miracle to me that he should have completed what he was doing, collected his party into the car and set off in time to intercept our departure. You may imagine our astonishment and delight to become aware of him in the car, joining his hands in a last farewell to us smiling through the window until he was nearly out of sight along the Sirsa road, whilst we went in a diagonally opposite direction to Ferozepur.

22nd February

Here in Ferozepur we have been leading the typical life of a large cantonment in India. Usha's husband is the brigade area commander here and has extended a most kindly welcome to us. I feel very much at home here having spent the better part of my life, during the winter months, in similar cantonments, in a succession of houses closely resembling this: large, cool bungalows, old and solidly built, with lofty ceilings lit by clerestory windows, situated in vast compounds and surrounded by shade trees and pleasant flower gardens and connected by quiet, well-kept clean roads, and a few local shops with the city a short distance away. It is a most comfortable life in winter, but blazing hot in summer, and most of the wives and families try to get away for some months at that time to nearby hill stations.

Nearly every evening we go for a drive or a walk in the countryside. During one of these walks Usha related an interesting incident which occurred in the lifetime of our Master, Maharaj Sawan Singh Ji. An old lady who lived in the Punjab had collected the money to repay a debt she had contracted. Being a careful soul and not willing to trust what represented a large sum to her to such a modern contraption as the post, she determined to pay her creditor in person. She set off on a rail journey involving a change of trains and unfortunately missed her connection. As night was falling and there was no train till morning and no suitable accommodation at the station, she asked a porter where she could find lodgings for the night. He gave her a lantern and directed her to a friend's house in the nearby village. Here she spent the night and, returning to the station in time to catch her train the next morning, was distressed to find that she could not locate her benefactor of the previous night.

She continued her journey and, on examining the lantern, found a label attached which read 'Dera Baba Jaimal Singh, Beas'. She made enquiries of her fellow passengers and ascertained that Beas was on her way. Having time on her hands, she determined to break the journey and return the lantern to its owner. As she entered the Dera, a satsang was in progress and she stopped to listen. To her surprise she recognized in the gentleman conducting the satsang her friend the porter and the owner of the lamp. After the satsang she returned it to him thanking him for his kindness. Smiling, he replied, to her surprise: "You must be mistaken, everybody here will tell you that I never left the Dera yesterday!" Realizing then the significance of what had happened to her, she begged for and later received Nam from him.

23rd February

23rd February

Something of the glory of those two days in Fazilka was renewed in our minds this morning when Mrs Diwan, who had called, began to recall the satsang and sing the shabd *"Saahib ke darbaar meŋ keval bhakti piyaar"* (Love alone counts in the court of the Lord) used on the second day we were there. We talked about it for a time and tried to memorize the tune *(rag)*. She added a fascinating footnote to the story of Shabri, the poor tribal devotee, who in a previous incarnation had been so lovely and dainty a princess that her hand had been sought in marriage by many suitors and a great deal of violence and bloodshed had resulted. Her distress at this was so great that she begged the Lord that in her next life she might be born poor and ill-favoured so that she might devote herself undisturbed to his worship, hence her condition at the time of Ram's visit.

By the 24th, Bea and I returned to Beas by train and were unexpectedly met at Kapurthala by Mr Ahluwalia and Diwan Daryai Lal Sahib, literally plucked off the train and taken by car—a merry party—to Beas.

26th February

Yesterday after satsang when we went to retrieve our shoes (it being common practice to remove them before satsang), nearby lay a strange insect about three inches long with a horny back, wings stiffly folded and large protuberant eyes, for all the world like an enormous cockroach, except that it seemed very sluggish, a most repulsive creature—right against the plinth upon which the satsang had just been given. We were examining it with wonder and some distaste, when one of the women standing nearby said: "It also has been attending satsang." Another soul, we then thought, like ourselves, only unfortunate enough to be subjected to the strange karma of being in such a body. Sympathy and pity for its lowly state filled our hearts and caused us to realize that we should be very understanding of all God's creatures and have a sense of kinship with all that lives.

To hark back again to Fazilka, Captain Diwan gave Bea the following record of a conversation between questioners, not yet initiated, and Maharaj Ji. The interview took place during his stay at the Canal Rest House.

Questioner: "Is there a God? Can it be proved logically and scientifically that God exists? If so, how?"

Maharaj Ji: "Yes, God is everywhere. What you people call science I know not! After all, what are the logic and sciences of this universe? All of them which we come to learn are reflections of the mind. The mind with its deliberations and reflections is limited, and logic and science are its output. God is a much higher entity than mind is capable of perceiving. To realize, know and contact him one needs higher faculties or sciences (if one may call them such) than the sciences of this world."

Questioner: "How can one know that God exists everywhere and realize or reach him?"

Maharaj Ji: "To give one an opportunity to be able to develop that faculty or science to know him and realize him is in the hands of God. He gives to whomsoever he wishes the knowledge of God, and he has his own ways of doing so. Once he makes a person his own, it becomes inevitable for that person to know God, and all that is connected with this higher science of the soul."

Dera Reunion

5th March

Maharaj Ji returned on 28th February very late and the Dera inhabitants were bidden to darshan by lamplight. A petrol vapour lamp was placed on the dais near him and hymns were sung. For his audience it was a most moving moment. At such times very often the Master's face is not expressive of human emotion but it is very 'alive' and his eyes travel to each individual in the audience much as a good shepherd might count his flock and note each one's well-being.

There are some wonderful similes he often gives in satsang. One is of a child, holding onto his father's finger and being taken to a fair. "Look how the child enjoys the pageant at a fair, says Maharaj Ji. "His eyes go round with wonder at the booths and roundabouts, the colours and the lights. But supposing his little hand slips from its grasp on the father's finger and he becomes separated from the warm comfort of his presence. The child's pleasure is shattered and his mind is racked with distress. He knows then in a flash that his happiness is not due to the show but is dependent on his father's presence. In like manner the soul, when it is in contact with its Creator, is full of appreciation of his work and joy in his company, but let its hand but slip from the finger of the Almighty, how full of trouble and woe it is!"

Then there is a graphic simile of the sounds one hears on going within on one's journey to Sach Khand. He says to think of a river flowing from its source to the sea. When it flows down a gorge between rocks, the sound produced is quite different from that heard when it flows over a cataract or when it hurls itself down a precipice in a waterfall, and different again when flowing peacefully across a plain or when it finally joins the ocean.

The day of the March satsang dawned wet and cold. It had been pouring all night and our lawn and that of the Rani ki Kothi next door was a 'lake'. We felt so inadequate and weak both in purpose and in our bodies when we were carried in a car to the satsang ghar for the meeting whilst the Indian sangat 'paddled' there in their bare feet with little or no protection from the pouring rain. The hall was absolutely crammed full, the balconies looking dangerously packed and doors wide, with people standing on chairs and on each other's shoulders at the doors and out into the verandahs. Over twenty thousand of them, Khanna Sahib said, and they had all had adequate shelter for the night. They can apparently shelter eighty-five thousand at a time. Sometimes during the biggest bhandara in July in the rains, ten or twelve thousand are out all night in the rain if the crowds reach above the limit of the accommodation. They have to go in shifts to the langar for their meals as there also shelter is limited. They have talked of roofing in the field where the bhandaras are held, but apparently it would have proved too costly.[*]

In his satsang the Master said: "We need a medicine which will stop our feverish and aimless wandering in this world, and if there is anyone who can minister to our long drawn-out spiritual malady, it is the Satguru. The attainment of inner vision and manifestation of the Guru's form within are the most important stages in the redemption of our emaciated spiritual faculties, chained as they are to the mind's chariot. The celestial sun with all its radiance, of which

---

[*] Adequate arrangements now exist to provide food and shelter for several hundred thousand people. [Editor]

the Master gives a hint, resides within us. Just ponder: what goes with us when we pass out of this world? Neither mother, nor father, nor children, nor possessions accompany us to the other world. Even our body that we nurture so meticulously remains behind to return to dust and ashes. Still we do not awaken to the reality that the Master and Nam alone are our unfailing friends both here and beyond, while others are fair-weather associates and in reality our enemies in disguise. Our true relation is he who remains with us through thick and thin. Such a one is only our Master who is with us here and hereafter. Others are false, time-servers, attached to us with bonds of selfishness. Satguru and Nam last through death."

The Master asks us to consider what we should then seek—the gratification of sensual desires or the fulfilment of our spiritual aspirations? Between the two scales of the balance, the heavier one will invariably prevail. Our entire life is spent in rearing children, in serving our family, in amassing wealth, in looking after our physical comforts, but we do nothing in pursuit of our real interest. Throughout our life we remain beasts of burden and forget the purpose for which this human form was given. We gamble away our precious moments granted us for the liberation of the soul, and waste twenty-two thousand breaths daily out of our allotted reserve. What could be a more reckless dissipation of our resources? Carry out your worldly tasks, but keep your mind in simran, for it is free and can be turned to good account by the repetition of God's Name. This does not cost a penny. It is the easiest thing to do in comparison with the extent of the reward, for the darkness of ages gives way to radiant light.

True Masters earn their own living—they take nothing from their followers for themselves—and they offer us release from eternal bondage. Yet history records only too vividly the treatment we have meted out to these saviours. They have been slighted, maligned, opposed and persecuted. Christ, Mansur, Shams Tabrizi, Guru Arjan Dev, Guru Teg Bahadur and Sarmad came to redeem us and we tortured or slew them. What heights of sheer ingratitude when their work is only to teach us God-realization, coming as they do on a mission of mercy and demanding no recompense for it. They do not ask us to change our way of life. All they ask is for devotion with which to remove the blinding screen that divides us from them. How sad it is if we get a free service and do not avail ourselves of it.

Pondering on this I thought: Just let me watch my own mind for a minute. It drifts about, hungrily manipulating its own actions and those of others to feed one worldly obsession or another, with little panic crises of running wild like a mad thing when my ego is roughly touched. It behaves like this because it is untrained to stand still for a minute to look through the bars of my cage and see the one who waits to allay this hunger with heavenly food. Really, at best, I am no better than a glorified animal, caged in my mind, without the sense to take advantage of the celestial banquet he is offering.

This evening the man they call 'Maulana Rum' (after the 13th century Persian poet and Master of that name, also known as Rumi) came at our request with a friend to chant the poet's verses and to translate and explain them. The passage he quoted ran as follows: The poet was sitting, meditating when Satan began to tempt him. Satan said, "Why do you continue to pray to the Lord, oh poet? Have you seen him or has he ever answered your prayer? Why are you wasting your time?"

So Rumi thought, "He is right! I have never seen him and he has not responded to my importunities." So he stopped meditating.

One day soon afterwards an angel appeared to him and said, "Why have you ceased to pray? God has not heard you pray lately."

The poet responded, "Why should I pray? I do not even know whether God exists; I have never seen him and he never answers my prayers."

The angel then replied, "Where do you think the desire to pray comes from? It only comes to you by favour of the Lord. If he did not will it, you would not even exist, let alone have the desire to pray."

Shopping Interval

7th March

Yesterday, having received permission to go, we went shopping to Amritsar, catching the morning bus which runs from Beas village, having missed an earlier one (8:30 a.m. summer timetable, 9:00 a.m. in winter) because of the change-over to the summer schedule. We therefore took a horse-

drawn conveyance *(tonga)* to Beas village. Not every bus, however, runs to Amritsar from there; we caught the wrong one
and had to change about a mile down the road. We shopped
during the morning, had lunch at quite a good restaurant
(there were two—the Nectar and the Aroma—that serve good
Western meals with plenty for a satsangi to choose from), and
after concluding our shopping we visited the local satsang
ghar, a fine place on its own grounds with a caretaker and his
family living there. We were back by 6:00 p.m. in time for
bhajan, having caught what purported to be the 4:30 bus,
but which left about fifteen minutes late. This bus also comes
right into the Dera, most others stopping at Beas village.

Holi

This morning the satsang given by Gurbachan Singh
was a delightful surprise as it started with a synopsis in English and the rest was more than usually interspersed with
English phrases. As it is approaching the time when the festival of Holi will be celebrated, the satsang was based on the
true interpretation of it. It was explained how the festival
originated from the inner planes. The soul, as it journeys upwards to Sach Khand, experiences beautiful colours, each
one connected with a separate plane until finally the soul
emerges, having gone through the range of prismatic colours,
in a brilliance of white light that we on this plane cannot
appreciate.

Shoti

Here I must retrace my steps a bit to the 2nd March and recall a wonderful interview with Shoti. We had been taking coffee with him the previous two mornings and that day we had a session which I don't think Bea, Lemani and I will easily forget.

All that he said was spoken as his own personal reactions and opinions but their application was so general as to be worth setting down whilst still fresh in the mind, so I will write them as they occur to me, not necessarily in the order in which they came.

He spoke of his personal and very special relationship with his own Master, and grandfather, saying it was one of great frankness and spontaneity. He said he used to disagree vehemently with him sometimes. He was not afraid to ask for anything he wanted, having an absolute childlike faith that he would get it and being quite prepared to pay the price for having it, and it seemed invariably to come to pass. During the time he was an officer in the army, if he wanted to visit Beas he would ask the Master's permission, and if he said yes, come rain or shine, he would take leave. He seems to radiate this faith and act on it without hesitation or fear. Decide, he says, in your own mind clearly what you must do and if you have full faith in its veracity, it will undoubtedly come to pass. He stressed very strongly, however, that this was his personal approach and he could not guarantee its success in the case of other people. Not everyone is capable of Shoti's degree of faith!

He told a story in this connection of a hermit who lived across the river from a village and who relied for his food on a man's bringing it every day from the village. One day, after the monsoon broke, the man said to the hermit: "Every day I find it increasingly difficult to bring your food. If it should rain heavily tonight, although I would dearly like to come and will do my best, I may not be able to cross the river tomorrow." The hermit told him to have no fear, that all would go well. The next day and for many subsequent days he continued to deliver the food, in spite of the river being in full spate, to the amazement of his fellow villagers. When they exclaimed at his ability to continue his mission and asked him how he managed to do so as the river was now impassable, he said, "Well, I don't know how it occurs, but the hermit told me I would be able to bring him his food, so I just obeyed him and went straight over to him."

The village priest, keeping watch on him, saw that he walked over on the water. Realizing that through this miracle there might arise the possibility of his losing his flock to the hermit, he said to himself, "Where one has gone safely, another may follow!" and he too attempted the crossing.

"But", said Shoti, "he took the precaution of tying a rope around his waist to make doubly sure of himself, and lack of faith was his undoing for he was swept away and drowned."

He told us how he had courted his colonel's displeasure by refusing to eat meat in the mess and subsequently obtained an unheard-of dispensation from attending mess seven nights a week; and how, in spite of all rules being to the contrary, he obtained leave whilst on training for active service in Burma, for the present Master's wedding.

On one occasion he had a very remarkable escape from death. He was the railway transport officer at a certain station during a troubled time when a fracas broke out, a Muslim troublemaker suddenly going berserk, shooting indiscriminately and killing one or two people before anything could be done to stop him. Somebody warned Shoti who ran unarmed to deprive the man of his rifle. The latter fired at him and missed, killing somebody behind Shoti, and fired again at point-blank range, taking off the top of Shoti's thumb; Shoti said he stood in front of the man strangely certain that he could not be killed. The man next charged Shoti with a bayonet fixed in his rifle which Shoti managed to deflect at the last moment; it passed through his jacket, scratching him and drawing a little blood. At the same time someone else shot the man from the side with a revolver. A friend took Shoti out of the station and ran him straight to the hospital. A rumour followed that he had been killed, and his colonel was actually posting him as dead when the general who had received the true report intercepted the message. Already the rumour had reached his grandfather at Beas, but Burreh Maharaj Ji would not believe it. That evening Shoti took leave from the hospital and went to Beas, which was not far away, and was able to give the lie to the rumour.

The highlight of the whole conversation for all of us came about thus: Bea said, "Sometimes the Master seems to do things that some of us find inexplicable. Could you tell us why this should be?"

Shoti said, "That does happen. Sometimes he seems to act in a way that you think is entirely wrong and perhaps your opinion is shared by others and on occasions all the satsangis present think it wrong and say so. Then Maharaj Ji explains and convinces them that what had seemed wrong to them was really the only feasible solution because (as becomes apparent later) he could see the full implication of the whole problem and had foreseen, on another plane, that which they could not possibly know." Then he made a very memorable remark: "When we see flaws in a Master, it is because he is a mirror. When we look at him, we cannot, with our limited vision, comprehend his masterhood; all we see is a reflection of our incompleteness." (This makes me feel that it could be used as a very good yardstick of one's own progress, or rather, lack of progress.)

Regarding doubts which spring up in the mind at such times he said, "Before you are initiated, you have every right to question and criticize the Master and Sant Mat, but after initiation it is necessary for progress that you have complete faith in the Master and faith that he acts as he does because he has an overall understanding of the whole problem and you have only a limited vision."

Then again he stressed that what is said to suit the progress of one person cannot be applied to another. The whole relationship is an extremely personal one between Master and disciple. There is no room for jealousy, because what he does for A at the time he does it is not applicable to B at that moment of time, and, as neither A nor B are in a position to judge their relative heights, they cannot then judge what they

do or do not merit from Maharaj Ji, and they should therefore take what he gives absolutely without questioning it.
Maharaj Ji's relationship with each disciple, based on each
one's individual angle of development, makes complete nonsense of jealousy.

Another significant fact he told us was that although
general rules are laid down on our conduct in Sant Mat, after
a soul has reached a certain height the Master may break his
own rule in relation to that particular person. As an instance
of this he quoted Shadi (who had been in charge of all the
machinery at the Dera in Burreh Maharaj Ji's time). Shadi
said, "All this time spent in bhajan trying to reach the Master!
If you have true love for the Master, you shut your eyes and
in two minutes you are in Sach Khand."

Shoti had already told us how indulgent Hazur Maharaj Ji was to him in his requests for leave of absence from his
army unit for Dera functions. When Burreh Maharaj Ji passed
away and Sardar Bahadur succeeded him, Shoti asked him if
he could expect the same indulgences and Sardar Bahadur
said, "No, for he was a king and I am a beggar."

Shoti also said: "Everyone without exception is a very
nice person all the time if we use the right, the most loving
line of approach."

"Nothing can stand against love", said Lemani.

"Love is an emotion on this plane, hate is an emotion;
anyone capable of a great hate is also capable of a great love
(one thought, here, of Saint Paul's dislike of Christ which
turned to love in a single moment). It is only the indifferent
ones who are difficult to reach because of their lack of reaction."

He said when Baba Jaimal Singh told Burreh Maharaj Ji of his decision to make him his successor, Maharaj Sawan Singh said, "I cannot, at the same time, look after the sangat and my family properly. I will take on your sangat if you will take care of my family!" So in family matters he always referred problems to Baba Jaimal Singh.

One of us asked Shoti, "Would you ever want to be born again?"

He replied, "No, never. I could go tomorrow and have no regrets. Everything I do, I do thoroughly and well but without a sense of attachment."

I only wish the atmosphere of this talk, and Shoti's charm and radiant, assured and yet childlike simplicity could be reproduced. He really made one experience complete confidence and humility at the same moment.

His Will

'Maulana Rum' came around again this afternoon and for his satsang took the text: "Thy will be done".

The sage Bahlol is greeted in the street by a friend who says, "Can you tell me something of this God of whom you speak? You say that God and you are one. Can you explain this fact?"

The saint responds by explaining that every action he performs is completely governed by the fact that God in the form of the Sound Current is omnipresent in his body. This Sound Current is like a soldier obeying his general. God says 'come' or 'go' and the Sound Current produces the effect in the individual of coming or going; no one laughs or cries but by his will; no leaf falls but by its agency. In this street the order is given by the Lord that a certain person must die and the Sound Current is withdrawn from him and he dies. In another street the decree goes forth that in such a house a baby will be born and the Sound Current goes to that house and the child is made manifest. "If thou wishest me to come, I come; if thou orderest me to go, I go. Where thou art, there am I. If thou art not, then I do not exist. Thy will be done."

Then he told the story of the four queens whose husband, the king, was going on a visit from his kingdom in Persia to India. He asked three of the queens what they wished him to bring back for them as presents. The first said a bolt of fine muslin, the second said a beautiful pair of shoes, and so on; but he was not moved to ask the fourth wife what she wanted for she was plain and unattractive. But when he was about to leave, he thought: Well, she too is my wife and in all justice I should ask her as well, and this he did. To his amazement all she said was: "I only want you, yourself, in person." He thought: She is wiser, after all, than any one of the others. So he went quietly on his journey and completed all his missions, and when he came back he went to the palace of the fourth queen and presented her with all the presents that the other queens had asked for, and furthermore took up his abode in her palace.

The three senior queens were dumbfounded and asked, "Why has this come to pass? She is ugly and ill-favoured, what has she done to deserve having our position?"

The king, hearing their complaints, told them: "All she wanted was to have me, so automatically she obtains all that I possess!"

Another story related by 'Maulana Rum' was as follows: A young man sat upon the top of a high wall at the foot of which ran a stream of clear pure water. He was very thirsty but the stream was deep and he had no way of getting down to the water, nor had he anything with which to draw the water up to his mouth. For the moment he was nonplussed. What was he to do? Having searched his mind for ideas, he took a brick from off the wall and threw it down into the stream below him. The water splashed up with a loud noise: "Garumph!"

"Why, my friend", remonstrated the stream in hurt tones, "do you throw stones at me?"

"In the first place," said the youth, "I am enchanted by the sound made by the stone falling into your depths, and secondly, by my action I am bringing myself nearer to you by demolishing this wall (of ego)."

Unless we descend from our wall of selfishness or ego, we do not appreciate the voice of the Master—the Sound Current—or what he says.

Then the disciple says, "Master, dear Master, give me pain. It is only when I have suffering that I remember you. Oh! Master, take over this body and this life. Do everything for me."

Bhajan can make people understand the truth far more thoroughly than the Bible or the Koran.

'Maulana Rum's' third satsang was about a young man who, travelling in a mountainous region, met Christ, who appeared to be running away from someone. The man asked him, "Lord, from whom do you escape? There appears to be no one, no enemy behind you." The Master continued on his way and made no reply and the young man running after him repeated his question.

Then Christ replied, "I am running away from a fool!"

The man said, "But are you not that Christ who, taking a handful of dust and throwing it up in the air can cause it to turn into live birds? Are you not he who brings the dead to life? Why are you afraid of a fool?"

"I am the man you speak of", said Christ.

"Why then", persisted the young man, "are you afraid of a fool? Can you not give him the same Nam as you give to other men, and so transform him?"

"I can initiate the deaf and the blind, cause the mountains to arise and go to another place or raise the dead to life, but I can have no dealings with a fool! One can have contact with a fool a hundred times without any effect. His heart is like stone, his life like sand. Upon him the Sound Current has no effect."

"Why then could you not cure this foolishness?"

"The blind and the deaf could cure themselves but foolishness is the will of the Lord so that the man who suffers from it does not come in contact with the Sound Current. The deaf and the blind are objects of pity, but there is no panacea for the foolish. Therefore, my dear friend, please hear me and avoid foolishness, (the foolish attachment to the people and things of this world) for contact with it will contaminate you and lead you onto the wrong path. Air dries up water little by little. Similarly, the foolishness of the world dries up spirituality."

Christ, 'Maulana Rum' tells us, was, of course not afraid of the fool, he was only giving us a graphic lesson.

In the next story, the poet illustrates how dangerous the questions 'How?' and 'Why?' can be. Sukman, his disciple, asked that he be given the power of a prophet and he replied that this was not advisable as yet. Instead, Sukman should go and become the servant of the great King David. So he went to the king's palace only to find him hard at work, doing blacksmith's work. He was curious as to what he was busy making, but restrained himself, thinking: "Don't ask, be quiet." Then he perceived that the king was making a suit of armour. Again he was tempted to enquire why he was making it and again he bade his mind, "Sit down, be quiet and have patience!" However temptation again came to him and he questioned himself thus, "Why not ask and have a quick settlement of my curiosity?" but his soul replied that he would not be given the real, the deep, significant reply even if he asked a hundred questions, so he kept quiet.

After some time, the work being completed, David gave Sukman the coat of mail and said, "This armour is invincible it will give you complete protection in battle. It is the coat of patience which keeps away anxiety. It is the touchstone which converts brass into gold. Always keep quiet and have patience and everything will come your way. Do not rail at the Lord, 'Why? Why this? Why that?' Have faith!"

Why do I not get results in my bhajan?
The Lord knows best!
Have faith and patience!

8ᵗʰ *March*

This morning's conversation at the breakfast table:

A: "What day is it today?"
B: "I don't exactly know."
C: "Wednesday, I think."
A: "No, I think it's Thursday the 8ᵗʰ."
B: "Well, Maharaj Ji came back on Sunday."
D: "I don't even know the year!"
A: "No, but seriously, let us look at the calendar!
    (Goes over to the wall calendar and returns
    mystified.) Sunday, the 8ᵗʰ of April! How can
    that be! Maharaj Ji came back on a Sunday."
B: "Silly, this is March."
A: "Ah, that explains it (looks again). Thursday,
    the 8ᵗʰ of March."

What a happy state to be in! A glorified Shangri-La!

9ᵗʰ *March*

Today we had an interview with Diwan Sahib Daryai
Lal, Maharaj Ji's private secretary for Western correspond-
ence, a member of the Dera Committee and a satsangi since
1910, a dear humble person who strongly reminds me of
Rai Sahib Harnarayan, at one time secretary to Maharaj Sawan
Singh.

Bea asked him how one could differentiate between
mind and soul. He recalled asking Burreh Maharaj Ji this
same question and the Master took him into his bathroom
where there stood a tub full of water in the sun, throwing a

reflection of the sun on the ceiling above. "That reflection", said the Master, "is like the mind—it is only a vague likeness of the original—the soul."

20th March

Today the Dera awoke once more as Maharaj Ji returned from a tour to Calcutta. At two o'clock in the afternoon we were told he had arrived and at 3:30 we went for public darshan followed by a little private spell with him for us Westerners and one or two Indians in his beautiful garden. A bauhinia tree was in full bloom dripping its pale cyclamen-coloured blossoms on the path below from the clustered boughs. Over the entrance arch were two creepers in bloom— a blood red bougainvillaea and a petrea with long trails of wisteria-like flowers and pale yellow-green leaves. The whole garden was banked with flowers and full of the scent of sweet peas and orange blossoms, and the lawns would have easily graced an English garden for size and abundance of greenery.

For days now our curiosity has been aroused, as a bullock-cart has been bringing great logs of wood to a site near the guest house and today we learnt the reason—to feed the brick-kiln oven. After leaving Maharaj Ji's garden we went over to the brick fields to witness the ceremony performed before the first bake of the year. The kiln itself is a large open rectangle sunk in a mound of brick rubble. Half of it is used at a time, and we went into the empty half by an entrance cut in the side of the mound. A block of unbaked bricks filled the other half of the kiln to its full height—about ten feet. From the top of the block two black chimney stacks pro-

truded centrally, held in position by wire stays, while at intervals shafts ran the length of the block at its base. These
shafts were roughly packed with sticks and twigs and a man
put a 'fire lighter' composed of a cow-dung cake dipped in
paraffin into the entrance of each shaft. A little traditional
ceremony was then solemnized; one of the workers (who are
not satsangis) dipped his hand in red dye standing nearby,
ready in a dish, and pressed the impression of his hand in
colour onto the topmost layer of bricks over each furnace
shaft—all this, while the crowd grew, Maharaj Ji having not
yet arrived. The audience was mainly gathered on the banks
above, with a few people down in the empty rectangle where
I was standing. Suddenly Maharaj Ji appeared in the entrance
smiling at me with great sweetness. These unexpected appearances, smiling, turn one's heart over with the poignancy
of their sweetness and radiance.

Once or twice before I have mentioned the impact of
one's becoming unexpectedly aware of the Master's presence,
having been at one moment preoccupied with the routine aspect of living and at the next, vitally alive to the intense joy
of beholding him—an elevation of spirit that imbues him
with (or, more likely he inspires one to feel) an indescribably
shining quality of love and affection. Guru Ram Das describes
it so well when he says, "My heart leaps up when I behold
my Satguru." This is what is missing when one does not have
a living Master. One cannot otherwise have the very personal
contact, necessary on this plane, to electrify one's heavy being
into such an obsession for the Satguru that it wipes out all
the other attractions of earthly merit which have proved so

fatally alluring through all one's lives of banishment from this other love.

Maharaj Ji stood for many minutes with eyes closed and head bowed, facing the brick wall, and one thought of the blessing being poured into those bricks, and the many thousands coming from the kiln in this year's work, enclosing the places in which many of us may live in future years, encompassing the gardens in which we and many thousands to come may walk and take their pleasure, the bricks that will go to building a huge new water tower which, we hear, is proposed as a part of this year's constructional plan, the water from which all who come here will drink and use. The streets are also to be rebricked and many of us will walk on his blessing. It made one realize that one cannot move here without breathing blessed, truly blessed, air. All the bricks of past bakings in the present buildings are little rectangles of singing blessed clay. Why is one so deaf and blind to it all? It encourages one to lose no time in going and doing more and more bhajan to really 'see' what a place we are living in! Indeed, this raised an echo in my mind of Rumi's description of the building of a temple in Jerusalem by King Solomon. "In his structures were seen magnificence. They were not frigid, dull and lifeless like any other buildings. Right from the first, every stone that was broken off from the mountain was eager to be quarried, a light was shining from the mortar, stones were coming without a carrier, and those doors and walls have become living."

Only those who truly love can see such vibrations in the Lord's construction; advanced souls must see all connected with a Satguru as one great song, which we lesser mortals perceive only very dimly or not at all.

How casually we, unbelievers that we are, eat the parshad he bestows on us. How crude its physical sweetness must seem, compared with its inner ambrosial sweetness and perfume. All the outer senses, we are told, have their mental and spiritual causes, which are the prototypes from which they have descended.

After the blessings, pathi Bhan Singh sang a shabd of invocation and then a man came forward proffering a long rod with a piece of sacking soaked in kerosene. Maharaj Ji was handed a box of matches, one of which he lit and set fire to the 'torch' which was then thrust by the man under the 'fire lighters' in each of the furnace openings. A cloud of smoke was soon billowing out across the countryside from the two tall chimney stacks.

The Master then went out quickly and over to a meadow nearby, closely followed by the crowd and people bearing big brass trays of browned sweet semolina used on these occasions for parshad. With a *charpoy* (lit. four legs; a woven rope bedstead) behind him, he stood and blessed the food and the people squatted, rank upon rank, around him on the grass. He then sat on the bedstead, and we happy ones beside him ate of his blessing. Dr Randolph Stone said, "This scene might all have been taken straight out of the Bible", and I thought: Yes, the feeding of the multitude, his disciples around their beloved Lord, the age-old countryside around us and the bank of the river in the background, and flocks grazing, with their shepherd not far away.

Bea and I came back to the guest house and looked back on the scene from a balcony: the brickfield, now deserted with its smoking stacks, the huge plain with fields, scrub river sands and a far tree-lined shore running in great bands of pearl across it; still further away to the north-east, soaring up and running along its breadth like a vast frieze were the Himalayas, with a bank of cumulus clouds, pink in the sunset; behind them a higher, absolutely flat layer of creamy stratus, and crowning all, the silver disc of the full moon. It was an unbelievable sight, as though one were looking into an astral heaven. The siren sounded, long and clear, bidding us to bhajan.

This morning we had an interesting session of questions. Bea asked, "What is imagination and how does it differ from intuition?"

Maharaj Ji said, "They are both of the mind, one more refined than the other. Imagination is more of that which we know and with which we are familiar, while intuition reaches up to the soul to draw on it but is still, nevertheless, the mind working."

"Imagination", said Mr. Khanna, "is born of desire, as one might conjure up castles in the air."

"Maharaj Ji, in reincarnation can a woman be born again as a man or must she forever be condemned to womanhood? I have heard that a man may step down to womanhood but once there, never again become a man. Is this true?"

"No, there is no truth in it. A man may come back as a woman, and a woman as a man, according to their karma. Sex ceases to exist above the mind regions anyway." Laughingly, he said: "There are people who say that women cannot go to Sach Khand, but this is not true. In the writings of saints (who are mostly men) you read such statements as 'Woman is the downfall of man.' But in the case of women, the same is implied of the opposite sex."

23rd March

Yesterday whilst we were sitting with Maharaj Ji after satsang, his servant came out of his house holding an exhausted sparrow in his hand and said it had been flying around in such a panic that finally it had fallen stunned to the ground. Maharaj Ji looked long at it lying in the man's hand, then told him to put it up on the sweet pea props. It looked very unsteady and somebody said it might fall out. Maharaj Ji said, "No, it will be all right", and one thought of the biblical quotation: "Are not two sparrows sold for a farthing? and one of them shall not fall on the ground without your Father. But the very hairs of your head are all numbered. Fear ye not therefore, ye are of more value than many sparrows" *(Matthew 10:29–31).*

Yesterday I had an appointment with him at seva so I stood up on the guest house top verandah to watch for him going by, so that I would not keep him waiting. Whilst watching the road outside, I saw a little old blind man, feeling his way to the site where seva was to be held. Faithfully every day he goes to do his stint, finding his own way everywhere. Just then, I espied Maharaj Ji coming along the road alone, except for Manohar, his personal servant. I hurried down and followed a little in the rear and presently they came abreast of the blind man, both of them not talking and no one else within earshot. At the same instant I marvelled to see the blind man half turn and, falling on his knees, prostrate himself at Maharaj Ji's feet. Maharaj Ji greeted him and talked a little and then passed on. How did that man guess the Master was there?

Karma
(Cause and Effect, Action and Reaction)

My understanding of Punjabi must be improving for at this morning's satsang based on one of Soami Ji's shabds, I was able, to my great joy and benefit, to understand nearly all that Maharaj Ji said, without assistance from others.

He said that in this life of violent contrasts, nothing is constant, not even pain lasts, and all of us are greatly confused. Soami Ji says he feels sorry for people of this world who are like castaways afloat on an ocean, the depth of which they do not know. Their boats are unseaworthy and the weather is inclement so they founder and drown. Although the soul has gone all the round of the lives of eight million, four hundred thousand kinds of creatures, it never learns that it is involved in an illusion of misery and pain. Look in the hospitals, go into the law courts, enter the prisons and see the travail people are suffering. People fight each other and are killed by the millions and in their turn they slaughter animals and birds for food and sport, never heeding their agony and cries for mercy. There is a reckoning however, after each life when the soul goes into the courts of the Lord and justice is meted out. Man, this creature made in God's image, has no pleasure in his existence, only constant pain.

Soami Ji said there is a way by which all this can be avoided. Imagine that you are in a fort with no doors and you wish to gather around you all that will ensure your happiness. How can you go and acquire it? There is no exit from this fort. Only by making a door in its wall can you go out and get the treasure with which to embellish your fort. Similarly the soul must find a way out of the fortress of the body and mingle with the ocean of spirit. The only bliss it can obtain is in merging with this ocean. Why then suffer? It remains for the soul to be taught the direction it must take. The Lord put a treasure within us and locked it up and removed the key and only he can give us back this key which is Nam.

The water diviner searching for a well in a ruined city does not dig for water. He goes to the old well among the decayed habitations and causes it to be uncovered. So the saints all use the same method in revealing the spirit of Nam to their elect.

This wealth of which they speak lies in the upper part of the head above the point between the eyes starting in the area known as the third eye. The wealth of the world lies in the area between the soles of the feet and the physical eyes, and in this part of the body, which only reaches out into the physical world, there is no peace.

Go then, and collect your attention within this upper realm of the body. Knock at the door which lies therein and in the words of Christ, it will be opened unto you. The real nectar of life lies here. This is the periphery of this magnetic field of spiritual power.

A soul that has descended into the depths has to fight its way back through myriad births with the greatest of difficulty, and within the short space of one human life he has to step firmly onto the path of salvation or else fall again into the possibility of another cycle of eighty-four lakhs,* blind and dumb to his divine origin. Therefore be warned and devote this human life to its true purpose. People are brought before the Master like coins before the coin tester. They come into the ante-room of his treasury, the true ones being put into his bank and the false, discarded.

Soami Ji asks us to consider what type of worship is required to burn our karma. There is no other method except to retrace the way by which we came, through the eye centre. The only method of ascertaining where our true home lies is by listening and holding onto the divine melody, the unstruck music within, so unlike our worldly orchestras which play and then cease, having drawn us, by their play on our emotions, back into the lure of the senses; but Shabd, the unstruck music, is always there within, therefore connect your body currents with it and ride on it to salvation.

Soami Ji then describes the three kinds of karma. The first is fate karma or *pralabdh,* which, like a crop of wheat sown in the last life, produces grain to be reaped in this life. This type of karma has to be undergone. Therefore, says the saint, learn to endure it patiently, but it is easier to bear if we

---

* Refers to the eighty-four hundred thousand categories of life forms through which the soul may pass.

do our bhajan. The second is present karma or *kriyaman,* actions done in this life, which have to be reaped in future lives. The third is reserve karma or *sinchit,* which is taken on by the Master at our initiation and burnt when we reach the top of the third region at the moment when, having shed the mind, the soul—naked and free of encumbrances—discovers its oneness with all creation and cries, "I am That!"

A means of burning this karma is by performing the four types of seva:

Devotion with the body, that is, physical service, the doing of which enables one to realize the dignity and equality of man.

Devotion with wealth, that is, charity used for the benefit of others, which subdues attachment to mammon.

Devotion of mind, that is, taking it back to the focal point between the eyes and away from the plane of the senses and the intellect.

Surat and Shabd seva-attaching the soul *(surat)* to the Sound Current *(Shabd)* and merging the soul with it. This is obtained after the three above are completed, and as a result of them.

After translating to the European members, Khanna Sahib gave us a little talk on what the Master says about the use of kindness as opposed to force in connection with the teachings of Sant Mat. Maharaj Ji advocates that one should not try to discipline the mind by force. He quotes many examples, recalling what occurred to some of the rishis and munis of old. Indian legend tells how they spent many years in isolation, disciplining and restraining the mind, but when they came back into worldly life, they succumbed to the first major temptation they had, just as coals, when covered with ashes, will flare up with the first wind that blows. The snake in the snake-charmer's basket, says Maharaj Ji, is harmless only so long as he keeps the basket closed, but it still has not lost its venom and will use it to ill-effect as soon as the lid is removed. The only way to ensure one's safety from the snake is to extract the sacs of venom from its mouth; then one may safely wear it around one's neck.

Again, he says, one cannot reform a bad character merely by keeping him locked up in jail (a fact we are only just taking cognizance of in the penal systems of the West). One should attempt to use persuasion. Why try to force a beggar to give up his pennies? Offer him sovereigns and then he will gladly give you his pennies. If a young girl is asked to give up her love and attachment to her parents, home and childhood friends, she will find this impossible; but if she marries and has a home with her husband, all these other things will have no further attraction for her and she will gladly forego them.

In his garden this morning Maharaj Ji spoke of many things. I asked if he would be holding satsang in England and he said, "Yes, certainly the Indians would want one." We had heard, I said, that many South Africans and Americans may come to England as soon as they knew with certainty that he was visiting Europe. Maharaj Ji said they should always consider the advisability of coming to India in preference to meeting him in other countries not their own, as hotel accommodation was so difficult and expensive and the time he could give to them there was very limited. We all really

need to be in one spot to get the maximum benefit from his
company. In Beas, this is assured and the cost of living is nil.
He felt the expense of the journey would be more than offset by this fact.

We spoke of having another tape in English and he
promised to make one. We suggested one in both English
and Punjabi, but he said each satsang was forty-five minutes
long. If he did as we asked, it would mean having a tape ninety
minutes in length, and in his experience no audience remained
attentive for more than three-quarters of an hour at a stretch.

We asked him where the tapes were prepared and he
said, "Here, in this house." We recalled the beauty of the
tape with the bird sound in it, and a dog barking, and he
laughed and said, "Yes, we make the tapes at night now so
that there will be absolute quiet. There was no audience of
any sort present so that there should be no inadvertent cough-
ing or sneezing. Once", he recalled with glee, "the siren went
in the middle of a recording and we had to remake the tape!"

24ᵗʰ March

At this morning's garden session we were talking of an
impending satsang at Ludhiana, sixty miles from here and we
asked if we might go. The difficulty was in finding transport
for nine of us. Could we all squeeze into the jeep, or, if any
of us had to stay behind, how could we equitably decide who?
I suggested drawing lots and Maharaj Ji, with great tact said,
with a twinkle in his eye: "I will leave the method of choosing
entirely to you!" So we said if we had to fight it out between
ourselves, there might be only pieces left. "Well I have room

for two pieces", said Maharaj Ji. Somebody suggested that
with an outsize shoehorn it might be done, and so it stands
at that. The party leaves at seven o'clock tomorrow morning.

The Inner Sanctuary

Yesterday, as well as today, I have been permitted to
enter my Master's (Maharaj Sawan Singh's) quarters, and
what a radiant visit it has been on both occasions. I saw again
the room in which on a bright October afternoon in 1941 I
was initiated, and the couch upon which he had sat whilst
giving the instructions. Also we went into his bedroom and
saw his bed that has never again been slept on by anyone else
since he passed on. Sardar Bahadur's bed, too, is still kept in
an ante-room where he slept as a Master.

Mr Khanna told us a story of a visit he and some friends
paid to Sardar Bahadur who always kept open house. (Here
he digressed to say that on occasions he was known to meet
a guest in his garden and say to him: "Welcome, my friend,
I am so glad you have been able to come", and the man would
say, "But sir, I have been here for the last ten days!") Whilst
these guests were there, one of them so far forgot himself as
to appropriate one of the objects in the house. Another guest,
in his zeal, reported the matter to the police who, apprehend-
ing the man, brought him to the door of Sardar Bahadur's
house. Hearing the resulting conversation, Sardar Bahadur
ordered the man's immediate release, adding: "No one has
stolen anything from me; nothing in this house belongs to

me, it is all the Master's and is for the free use of anybody who wishes to take it." So the man was released forthwith.

Comparing our reactions after this visit, we were all agreed that of every place in the Dera, this house is most fraught with, for lack of a better description, vibrations of light and joy. How can I say what it means to those of us whose living associations with it are of the most sacred!

25th March

Today the party went with Maharaj Ji to Ludhiana. I was nervous about the journey of sixty miles and back, as my eyes were giving me some pain. Instead, as we stood in the Master's garden by the lily pool, having his darshan before he left with the others, Harjit asked if I would carry out my promise and teach her to cook English dishes. Of course I needed no second bidding and set my mind to work to concoct a menu that would be acceptable to Maharaj Ji, as he does not take sugar or starch in any quantity (starch-reduced flour is used, with no fried foods and very little fat or onions with his meals). With the other limitations we have, plus the fact that our British flavourings and patent ingredients are in short supply, or not available at all, it required careful thinking to select dishes that met all these restrictions, but with Harjit's guidance and inspiration from her cookery books, we managed a tolerable meal—Irish all-vegetable stew, another vegetable dish and a baked apple which met with—or so I was told later—his approval. This is proving of great value to me as a guide to what he may require when he comes to us in Britain.

26ᵗʰ March

Today was spent in Amritsar getting income tax clearance.

27ᵗʰ March

Another mutual cookery lesson for Harjit and me to-day. Whilst the final touches were being given to the meal, and my back was turned to the door, a voice said, "Aha! We have an English cook now!" For a second I did not appreciate who it was who spoke, and then once more experienced that wonderful feeling of amazed delight at being unexpectedly faced with our beloved! The whole kitchen was suddenly alight with laughter and happiness. Harjit insisted that I dine with them, though my one desire was: please let me only serve.

Maharaj Ji was in a cheerful mood. He said that we were bearing him off to England and when I said I only wished he was coming with us, he said, "Well, practically I am coming with you", which, when you think about it, is quite the truth! He said today he had written to complete the bookings for his journey by way of Tehran (of the latter he said: "Persia was the ancient centre of great mystic knowledge; the Sufi movement was very strong there; their saints were very wonderful"), through the Middle East and Europe, to us in the United Kingdom, and home by way of Spain and Egypt.

Little Satsaṅgs

This afternoon we had another illuminating session with 'Maulana Rum.' I feel so grateful to Maharaj Ji for allowing us these little satsangs with him for he translates so vividly, getting faithfully to the heart of each precept and anecdote so that one is beguiled into an indelible remembrance of the lesson they teach—more effectively perhaps than if they were conveyed in a series of abstract statements.

Today he told us of the beggar who was roaming the streets naked with nothing to eat or drink and met a band of sumptuously clad servants of a rich man. These men were on their way to obtain purchases in the local bazaar and, being full of envy for their good fortune, the beggar, addressing his Master in his heart, said: "Oh my Lord, look how these people are parading themselves, dressed in the finest of raiment and well fed. *Their* Master knows how to look after those dependent on him. Why do you not follow his example and do likewise by your servants, such as I. Look how I roam penniless and trembling with the cold, for the weather is very bitter."

Now this beggar was proud at heart and had a great ego, for had he not the temerity to teach God a lesson? So the Lord said to him, "Dear friend! Are you taking the Lord to task? All you want are the external trappings that a servant of the king wears. You are praying for a coronet to wear on your head. Why do you not thank God instead for having a head? This is a much greater gift than any crown!"

Here 'Maulana' interrupted his translation to tell us the story of a woman who came to him crying, saying she was heartbroken and could not bear the loss of her only son, so he comforted her thus: "Think a moment! If your son, when he was a child, had been playing with his toys and you wanted him to come for his meal, and he refused because he was interested in his game and began to cry with frustration, how would you have dealt with the situation?"

She replied, "I would have taken the toys away from him, even if he cried, and he would soon have got over it; I would have reasoned that it was for his ultimate good to do so."

"Yes," he said, "that is what God is doing to you now. He has taken away your toy and presently he will give you the meal he has called you for, and then you will forget the sorrow the loss of your son has caused."

April Bhandara

31st March

The people are arriving for the April 2nd bhandara at an ever-increasing pace. From yesterday there have been two satsangs daily and the guest houses are filling and will be occupied to capacity by the 2nd. Every day a vast crowd assists at mitti seva and 'mountains' are being moved and 'valleys' filled in. The atmosphere is thick with dust, the lilt of singing voices and an indefinable sense of common purpose, joyful service and the desire to hurry to the spots where darshan may be had. Once there, we drag our feet and draw out the minutes as long as propriety and the pushing crowd will allow. It is strange how one fetches and carries quite heavy loads of earth all the while Maharaj Ji is in sight and how heavy the burden becomes when he finally leaves us and goes back into the Dera.

Yesterday, Bea heard that she was to accompany Maharaj Ji on his European tour as far as Germany and we all joined in rejoicing with her.

Today, for satsang, two shabds were taken, both of which are in the book *Light on Sant Mat*—first, a repetition of "Love alone counts in the court of the Lord" *(Saahib ke darbaar meŋ keval bhakti piyaar)* by Paltu Sahib; and second, "Cleanse thy heart's chamber for the beloved to come" *(Dil kaa hujraa saaf kar, jaanaaŋ ke aane ke liye)* by Tulsi Sahib. It is quite a good idea to catch the first line of the shabd the pathis sing, for very often they are in one or other of the books or other Sant Mat literature and are substantially what the Master says in Punjabi. Though they are often repeated, to the sangat they are as beloved—more so—than the words and music of a familiar and fragrant love song. The Master's personality lends them such a delicate freshness that the crowd, knowing what is coming next, goes half way to meet it.

What a dear, clear-eyed person Harjit, the Master's wife, is. She is a lesson in simple bright dignity and a helpmate for Maharaj Ji in every sense of the word. She has a very lively intelligence and is using it to train herself in every accomplishment that may prove useful to her as his hostess and in secretarial ways as well.

They have three children; Nirmal Jit, the eldest (Nimmi for short) and two sons, Jasbir Singh and Rana Ranbir Singh (whose pet names are Cuckoo and Rana). They all attend English schools in the hills.

2nd April

Life has moved very fast in these last few days and so I will jot down happenings as they occur to me. Today's satsang—the bhandara satsang in commemoration of Hazur Maharaj Sawan Singh's passing—lasted two hours. The crowds were enormous, beyond estimation by eye, but they say that the langar has an infallible method of being able to judge the numbers. The satsang shabd was "Our soul is in God and God is in us" *(aatam meh raam, raam meh aatam)* by Guru Nanak. During the discourse, Maharaj Ji spoke of the nature of the Sound Current. He said that Shabd is of two kinds: *varnaatmak* (spoken) and *dhunaatmak* (that which cannot be spoken or described). In describing the latter we can only give an approximation, by comparing it to its earthly equivalent, which is only a reflection of it. This Sound reverberates within us all but we cannot contact it until, at initiation, the Master connects us with the highest plane from whence it originates.

The very nature of this material world is such that it clothes and buries the living Sound in all the forms we know here. They are but reflections of their real selves and if we would know them truly then we must scale off this material covering by going within our own bodies and finding their unstruck music. Of all the beautiful forms we know here— even beautiful music—we would not waste a moment with them as we know them here, if we could hear the real Sound of which all this is a miserable reflection.

He also mentioned the necessity for cultivating the feeling of contentment with one's lot—living in the Lord's will, or *bhaanaa*. He explained the nature of *bhaanaa* at some length: calamity should not discourage us, nor should we be elated by worldly pleasures or associations—we are to do everything to the very best of our ability but the results are to be left entirely to God. Devotion to God should be for love of him and not for what he can give us. One is reminded here of the story of Paul Cezanne, the artist, who, when he had explored in full the subject he wished to paint, stood the resulting picture against the nearest bush and walked away having lost interest in it with the last brush stroke. So that they might survive, his wife would follow him around collecting up his creations surreptitiously and sell them to some purpose.

This afternoon, as is customary following the April bhandara, the annual general meeting of the Beas Committee was held and we were asked to attend a little tea party in Maharaj Ji's garden afterwards. As I am leaving tonight, alas, I took the opportunity of saying goodbye to many very dear Dera friends. "You have become like one of us", said Daryai Lal, that wise, quiet man, whose work brings him so close to the Master and of whose gentle wisdom we so often drank.

Only this morning at the Western satsang I asked to be enlightened about the real nature and manner of accumulating *sinchit* or reserve karma. If the last life's *kriyaman* or new karma becomes this life's *pralabdh* or fate karma, how does *sinchit* fit into this scheme? Perhaps I phrased it vaguely, for Maharaj Ji only answered, "It is reserve karma", or perhaps being such a busy day, time pressed; but as so often happens on these occasions, Maharaj Ji sensed my desire for more information and one of his aides became his mouthpiece.

Daryai Lal detained me as we were going out and said, "This illustration may serve to answer your question. If you are a meat-eater and kill and eat, say, five hundred fowls in a life-time, you cannot repay all that debt in the next life. Only one life may be repaid as *pralabdh* and the other four hundred and ninety-nine become *sinchit* karma", which I thought was a brilliant explanation of the position!

Taking Leave

After the party I went in to have my last 'darshan' as is customary, to receive parshad and to be given a striking por-trait of the Master. Maharaj Ji greeted me by saying, "So, you are going home!" with a twinkle in his eye.

So I said, "I am going, but I don't know about 'home'!" (Mentally I remember thinking: Where is 'home'?) He asked if I were going to be taken care of in Delhi and I told him I was travelling from Beas with Mrs Kamal Bagai who would look after me. Our Satguru then gave me his blessing and it was during this that I realized the truth of the saying that to serve a Guru (seva) is in truth to gain spiritual wealth for oneself. One can give nothing in return to him—he can cause sticks and stones to serve him as efficiently as any human being, and to their great benefit.

I felt no sadness this time at parting, only a great desire to go and serve.

Later, Kamal, her mother-in-law and I had a good jour-ney to Delhi and her hospitality to me there is one of my treasured memories. Our lives had been linked at many points before, without consciously knowing it, until this visit to Beas. She is an initiate of Baba Sawan Singh Maharaj and was especially close to him during his lifetime. He 'adopted' her after her father's death, and she was treated by him as one of his own family during his lifetime.

The journey back by way of Bombay, Karachi, Doha, Cairo, Rome, Frankfurt, and London, was easy though very tiring. The combination of being recently returned from such an environment and the quickness of aerial transport leaves one with a curious disembodied feeling which makes it difficult to settle back into one's daily round.

What can I say of my experiences? Whatever I write will be an understatement of my true impressions, but to those who may be pondering whether or not they should go to the Dera, I would so like to urge them not to hesitate one instant, but go, and go for as long as possible. Though I had visited Beas many times before, over a period of years, this last occasion was so rich in spiritual experience; so many ends were tied up, so many knots resolved, through personal association with the Master and his disciples over a reasonably long stay—roughly three months—and in the most propitious circumstances. I learnt so much from others that it has taught me the necessity for associating with fellow satsangis, for as often and as long as possible. Truly, by such association, longing and love for the Master is deeply engendered and one's bhajan is benefitted—the final criterion in deciding all action.

Radha Soami.

EPILOGUE

Epilogue

Some years ago we heard of a man who set foot on the moon, and there has lately been much speculation amongst the men of science as to how and whence came all the worlds floating about in our skies, rocks such as our world and worlds of fire such as our sun. Some have ruminated on the idea that all came into being in a big bang through a black hole like a shot fired by God through an immense celestial cannon.

All these speculations arise in the mind of living man. Why then does he not turn his spiritual power, the only known living power in this universe of ours, to searching inwardly, *inside* his own mind?

Never could we foretell with any accuracy how to read the behaviour of our future weather, until clever man devised a satellite rocket to fire out far above the bands of wind and cloud-forms in the sky. So why do we not sit and concentrate our soul power, firing it like that rocket, up into the uncharted layers of the inner sky? All the effects in our physical world come into being inside our heads, as internal vibrating concepts, which become concentrated into ideas like the blueprints of houses and aeroplanes being planned in the minds of their architects. So why not seek the origin of the infinitely finer vibration of our life force, back to our own foreheads

from where it issued? But having got there, we need a supreme
Saint to tell us how to rise above the darkness we then experience at that point, and who is expert enough to be trusted
to guide us through all that lies beyond it.

The spoken word can never take us along the road to
ultimate Eternity. As a child, listening to my schoolmates
gabbling the Lord's Prayer as quickly as possible so they could
go out to play, I used to wonder: Here we are, in a convent
dedicated to the religious life of worship of the Most High.
What then, does this prayer really mean? Child that I was, I
could find no answer. I thought: My mother, a Protestant,
prays: "Our Father *which* art in heaven"; and here in school,
Catholics say "Our Father *who* art in heaven", which means
they intimate he is a person. Is he out there, a kind fatherly
old gentleman, resting on a damp cloud; or is he some feeling inside me that is demanding my full attention?

When we grow up and find a Master, through habit we
carry these mundane ways of reasoning with us into our early
practice of Sant Mat. The outer form of the physical Satguru
is our target of worship and we strive with each other to show
who is the strongest in expressing our appreciation and respect for him only in the way our *earthly* senses perceive him.
Then if we leave his presence, or he goes away, time and space
make a gap that tends to dim our love through forgetfulness.
He seems to be telling us so clearly: Don't worship this earthly
form, this *who* that you have made of me. Go to that *which*,
that power of Shabd, the Holy Ghost inside your innermost
being that shines within you. Then I will always be present,
always available; now, and now, and now, a glorious hymn

of sound and light and life, of bliss and peace and joy within you, against which all the calamities and attractions of life in the world will pale into insignificance and disappear. Mankind is busy outside, searching like the scientists do in outer space for the black hole through which we came when creation began with a **BANG!** But, from the moment of initiation we can now look within much more convincingly through that black hole of our third eye, into a growing and widening awareness of timeless perception that no earthly words can convey.

Flora E. Wood
2000

Addresses for Information and Books

GUAM
Mrs. Hoori M. Sadhwani
115 Alupang Cove
241 Condo Lane, Tamuning 96911

HONG KONG
Mr. Manoj Sabnani
RSSB-HK, 3rd Floor, Eader Centre39-
41 Hankow Road,
Tsim Sha Tsui, Kowloon

JAPAN
Mr. Jani G. Mohinani
Radha Soami Satsang Beas
1-2-18 Nakajimadori
Aotani, Chuo-Ku
Kobe 651-0052

SOUTH KOREA,
TAIWAN, R.O.C.
Mr. Haresh Buxani
3rd floor, Eader Centre
39-41 Hankow Road
Tsim Sha Tsui
Kowloon, Hong Kong

NORTH AMERICA

CANADA
Mr. John Abel
#701-1012 Beach Avenue
Vancouver, B.C. V6E 1T7

Mrs. Meena Khanna
149 Elton Park Road
Oakville, Ontario L6J 4C2

MEXICO
Dr. Hector Esponda
RSSB-Mexico
Circuito Universidad 360
(In front of Vista Vallarta Golf Club)
Puerto Vallarta, Jalisco 48290

UNITED STATES
Mr. Hank Muller
1900 North Loop West, Suite 500
Houston, TX 77018

Dr. Vincent P. Savarese
2550 Pequeno Circle
Palm Springs, CA 92264

Science of the Soul Study Center
2415 East Washington Street
Petaluma, CA 94954

Dr. John Templer
114 Verdier Road
Beaufort, SC 29902-5440

Science of the Soul Study Center
4115 Gillespie Street
Fayetteville, NC 28306-9053

Dr. Frank E. Vogel
71 Old Farm Road
Concord, MA 01742

CARIBBEAN

FOR CARIBBEAN
Mr. Sean Finnigan
P. O. Box 2314
Port-au-Prince
Haiti, W. I.

BARBADOS
Mr. Deepak Nebhani
Radha Soami Satsang Beas
Lot No. 10, 5th Avenue
Belleville, St. Michael
Barbados, W. I.

CURACAO
Mr. Frank Claessen
La Quinta Villas 121
St. Catharina
Curacao, N. A.

GUYANA
Mrs. Rajni B. Manglani
A-80 Eping Avenue,
Bel Air Park,
Georgetown, Guyana

JAMAICA
Mrs. Shammi Khiani
P. O. Box 22
Montego Bay
Jamaica, W. I.

ST. MAARTEN
Mrs. Kanchan Mahbubani
R.S.S.B. Foundation
P. O. Box 978
Phillipsburg
St. Maarten, N. A.

SURINAME
Mr. Chandru Samtani
15 Venus Straat
Paramaribo
Suriname

TRINIDAD
Mr. Chandru Chatlani
20 Admiral Court
Westmoorings-by-Sea
Westmoorings
Trinidad, W. I.

CENTRAL AMERICA

BELIZE
Mrs. Chand Babani
5789 Goldson Avenue, Belize City

PANAMA
Mr. Deepak Dhanani
Altos Del Bosque
Residencial El Doral, Casa 195
Republica De Panama

SOUTH AMERICA

FOR SOUTH AMERICA
Mr. Hiro W. Balani
P.O. Box 486,
Malaga 29012, Spain

ARGENTINA
Mrs. Fabiana Shilton
Leiva 4363
Post Code 1427 Buenos Aires

BRAZIL
Mr. Willefort Leao
Rua Plinio Moscoso 1248
Edif. Sol de Verao, Apt. 201
40155-190, Salvador

CHILE
Mr. Vijay Harjani
Cosmos International S. A.
Manzana 5, Sitio 3
Iquique

COLOMBIA
Mrs. Emma Orozco
Calle 45, #99-25, Medellin

ECUADOR
Dr. Fernando Flores Villalva
Radha Soami Satsang Beas-Ecuador
Calle Marquez de Varela
Oe 3-68y Ave. America
P.O. Box 17-21-115, Quito

PERU
Mr. Carlos Fitts Villalva
P.O. Box 180658
Rinconada del Lago
1016-201 Lima

VENEZUELA
Mr. Jose Penaherrera
Calle "A", Residencias
Minarete, 9° Piso, Apto
91B, Urb.La Alameda,
Stafe, Caracas 1080

EUROPE

AUSTRIA
Mr. Hansjorg Hammerer
Sezenweingasse 10, Salzburg A-5020

BELGIUM
Mr. Piet J. E. Vosters
Driezenstraat 26
Turnhout 2300

BULGARIA
Mr. Emilio Saev
Foundation Radha Soami Satsang Beas
Bulgaria
P. O. Box 39, 8000 Bourgas

CYPRUS
Mr. Heraclis Achilleos
P. O. Box 29077, Nicosia 1035

CZECH REPUBLIC
Mr. Vladimir Skalsky
Maratkova 916,
420 00 Prague 411

DENMARK
Mr. Tony Sharma
Sven Dalsgaardsvej 33
DK-7430 Ikast

FINLAND
Ms. Anneli Wingfield
P. O. Box 1422
00101 Helsinki

FRANCE
Ct. Pierre de Proyart
7 Quai Voltaire,
Paris 75007

GERMANY
Mr. Rudolf Walberg
P. O. Box 1544
D-65800 Bad Soden / Taunus

GIBRALTAR
Mr. Sunder Mahtani
RSSB Charitable Trust Gibraltar
15 Rosia Road

GREECE
Mrs. Eleftheria Tsolaki
P.O. Box 35
Paleo Faliro 17503, Athens

ITALY
Mrs. Wilma Salvatori Torri
Via Bacchiglione 3, 00199 Rome

*THE NETHERLANDS
(HOLLAND)*
Radha Soami Satsang Beas - Nederland
Middenweg 145 E
1394 AH Nederhorst den Berg

NORWAY
Mr. Sohan Singh Mercy
St. Halvardsgt. 6
N-3015 Drammen

POLAND
Mr. Vinod Sharma
ul. 1go Sierpnia 36 B M-100
PL-02-134 Warszawa, Warsaw

PORTUGAL
Mrs. Sharda Lodhia
Rua Quinta Das Palmeiras, Lote 68
11° andar C, Oeiras 2780-145

ROMANIA
Mrs. Carmen Cismas
C.P. 6-12, Braila-810600

SLOVENIA
Mr. Marko Bedina
Brezje pri Trzicu 68, 4290 Trzic

SPAIN
Mr. J. W. Balani
Calle Panorama no. 15
Cerrado de Calderon
Malaga 29018

SWEDEN
Mr. Lennart Zachen
Norra Sonnarpsvägen 29
S-286 72 Asljunga

SWITZERLAND
Mr. Sebastian Zust-Bischof
Weissenrainstrasse 48
CH 8707 Uetikon am See (ZH)

UNITED KINGDOM
Mr. Narinder Singh Johal
Haynes Park Estate
Haynes, Bedford MK45 3BL

AFRICA

BENIN
Mr. Jaikumar T. Vaswani
01 Boite Postale 951,
Recette Principale, Cotonou

BOTSWANA
Dr. Krishan Lal Bhateja
P. O. Box 402539, Gaborone

GHANA
Mr. Murli Chatani
Radha Soami Satsang Beas
P. O. Box 3976, Accra

IVORY COAST
Mr. Konan N'Dri
08 Boite Postale 569
Abidjan 08

KENYA
Mr. Surinder Singh Ghir
P. O. Box 15134,
Langata 00509, Nairobi

LESOTHO
Mr. Sello Wilson Moseme
P. O. Box 750
Leribe 300

LIBYA (G.S.P.L.A.J.)
Mr. Roshan Lal
P.O. Box 38930, Bani Walid

MAURITIUS
Dr. I. Fagoonee
17 Manick Avenue
La Louise,
Quatre Bornes

NAMIBIA
Mrs. Jennifer Mary Carvill
P. O. Box 1258
Swakopmund 9000

NIGERIA
Mr. Nanik N. Balani
P.O. Box 5054, Lagos

RÉUNION
Ms. Marie-Lynn Marcel
5 Chemin 'Gonneau
Bernica, St Paul 97435

SIERRA LEONE
Mr. Kishore S. Mahboobani
82/88 Kissy Dock Yard,
P O Box 369, Freetown

SOUTH AFRICA
Mr. Gordon Clive Wilson
P. O. Box 47182, Greyville 4023

RSSB - SA
P.O. Box 5270
Cresta 2118

SWAZILAND
Mr. Peter Dunseith
P. O. Box 423, Mbabane

TANZANIA
Mr. D.N. Pandit
P.O. Box 1963
Dar-Es-Salaam

UGANDA
Mr. Sylvester Kakooza
Radha Soami Satsang Beas
P. O. Box 31381, Kampala

ZAMBIA
Mr. Chrispin Lwali
P.O. Box 12094
Chingola

ZIMBABWE
Mr. G.D. Wright
Pharmanova, P. O. Box 1726, Harare

MIDDLE EAST

BAHRAIN
Mr. Mangat Rai Rudra
Flat No. 12 Building No. 645
Road No. 2107
Manama 321

ISRAEL
Mr. Michael Yaniv
Moshav Sde Nitzan
D.N. Hanegev 85470

KUWAIT
Mr. Vijay Kumar
P. O. Box 1913, 13020 Safat

U.A.E.
Mr. Mohanlal Badlani
R.S.S.B. P.O. Box 37816,
Dubai

BOOKS ON THIS SCIENCE

SOAMI JI MAHARAJ
Sar Bachan Prose
Sar Bachan Poetry (Selections)

BABA JAIMAL SINGH
Spiritual Letters (to Hazur Maharaj Sawan Singh: 1896-1903)

MAHARAJ SAWAN SINGH
The Dawn of Light (letters to Western disciples: 1911-1934)
Discourses on Sant Mat
My Submission (introduction to Philosophy of the Masters)
Philosophy of the Masters (Gurmat Sidhant), in 5 volumes
    (an encyclopedia on the teachings of the Saints)
Spiritual Gems (letters to Western disciples: 1919-1948)
Tales of the Mystic East (as narrated in satsangs)

MAHARAJ JAGAT SINGH
The Science of the Soul (discourses and letters: 1948-1951)

MAHARAJ CHARAN SINGH
Die to Live (answers to questions on meditation)
Divine Light (discourses and letters: 1959-1964)
Light on Saint John
Light on Saint Matthew
Light on Sant Mat (discourses and letters: 1952-1958)
The Master Answers (to audiences in America: 1964)
The Path (first part of Divine Light)
Quest for Light (letters: 1965-1971)
Spiritual Discourses, in 2 volumes
Spiritual Heritage (from tape-recorded talks)
Thus Saith the Master (to audiences in America: 1970)

BOOKS ABOUT THE MASTERS
Call of the Great Master—Diwan Daryai Lal Kapur
Heaven on Earth—Diwan Daryai Lal Kapur
Treasure Beyond Measure—Shanti Sethi
With a Great Master in India—Julian P. Johnson
With the Three Masters, in 2 volumes—from the diary of
    Rai Sahib Munshi Ram

163

INTRODUCTION TO SPIRITUALITY

A Spiritual Primer—Hector Esponda Dubin
Honest Living: A Means to an End—M. F. Singh
The Inner Voice—Colonel C. W. Sanders
Liberation of the Soul—J. Stanley White
Life is Fair: The Law of Cause and Effect—Brian Hines

BOOKS ON MYSTICISM

A Treasury of Mystic Terms, Part I: The Principles of Mysticism
   (6 volumes)—John Davidson
The Holy Name: Mysticism in Judaism—Miriam Caravella
Yoga and the Bible—Joseph Leeming

BOOKS ON SANT MAT IN GENERAL

In Search of the Way—Flora E. Wood
Living Meditation: A Journey beyond Body and Mind
   —Hector Esponda Dubin
Message Divine—Shanti Sethi
The Mystic Philosophy of Sant Mat—Peter Fripp
Mysticism, The Spiritual Path, in 2 volumes—Lekh Raj Puri
The Path of the Masters—Julian P. Johnson
Radha Soami Teachings—Lekh Raj Puri
A Soul's Safari—Netta Pfeifer

MYSTICS OF THE EAST SERIES

Bulleh Shah—J. R. Puri and T. R. Shangari
Dadu, The Compassionate Mystic—K. N. Upadhyaya
Dariya Sahib, Saint of Bihar—K. N. Upadhyaya
Guru Nanak, His Mystic Teachings—J. R. Puri
Guru Ravidas, The Philosopher's Stone—K. N. Upadhyaya
Kabir, The Great Mystic—Isaac A. Ezekiel
Kabir, The Weaver of God's Name—V. K. Sethi
Mira, The Divine Lover—V. K. Sethi
Saint Namdev—J. R. Puri and V. K. Sethi
Saint Paltu—Isaac A. Ezekiel
Sarmad, Martyr to Love Divine—Isaac A. Ezekiel
Sultan Bahu—J. R. Puri and K. S. Khak
Tukaram, The Ceaseless Song of Devotion—C. Rajwade
Tulsi Sahib, Saint of Hathras—J. R. Puri and V. K. Sethi